MASTERING ESP32 PRACTICAL PROJECTS WITH ARDUINO IDE PROGRAMMING

From Basics to Advanced Techniques for Building Smart Devices with Arduino

By

Furuta Kimiko

TABLE OF CONTENTS

WHAT IS THIS PROJECT ABOUT

So I guess that you want to learn how to use the amazing ESP 32. Like me, you know about this powerful microcontroller and you're interested in using it in your projects. You've already used them in your projects, but you've hit a limitation. Perhaps your projects need more memory, more speed and more pinch. You've heard that the ESP 32 is a powerful microcontroller that can replace the Arduino with the ESP 32. You can get a lot more capacity to build more interesting projects almost for free. The problem is that the ESP 32 is not a plug in replacement for the Arduino. While it shares much of the edginess, programming and GPIO interfaces, you still need to learn the basics before you can deploy it. So you did what most of us do.

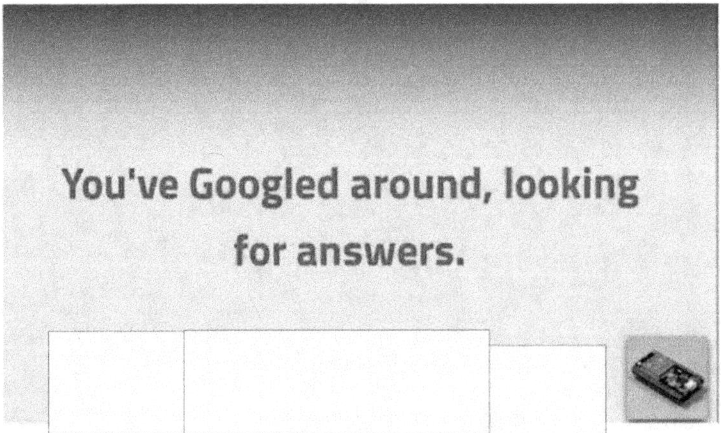

You've Googled around, looked around the Internet, looking for answers. If you've had enough of googling and you want to learn the ESP 32, then this quote is for you. Just too busy to waste time. You value quality content, you value time, and most importantly, you just want to get it right. In this project, you learn what is the ESP 32 and what are those various modules with a name? How are those modules scalable to ash in the form of development kits? What are the differences between the ESP 32 and the I do not and similarities? How can we use what we know from the Arduino to make things based on the ESP 52? How can we use the ESP 32BIOS to work with simple components like LEDs and buttons, but also to drive peripherals like sensors and motors? How can we set up the familiar Arduino IDP so that we can write programs for the ESP 32? You learn how to use the ESP 32 to drive motors, store data in nonvolatile memory and communicate with near-field devices and the Internet.

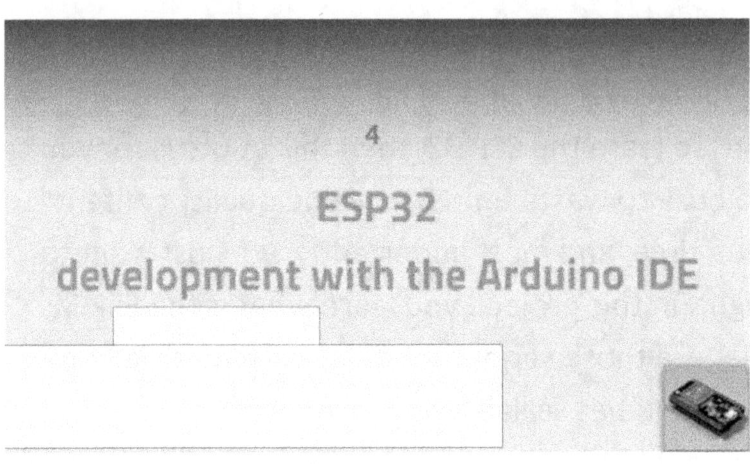
4
ESP32
development with the Arduino IDE

We've also included many humorous projects to demonstrate how to use capabilities such as your reading right? Classic Bluetooth, Bluetooth, low energy wi fi, digital analogue conversion, touch sensors and more. Larger projects will also show you how to create simple Internet of Things and Bluetooth applications to name just a few. If you're ready to learn more, please be sure to watch the following projects in this introductory section.

SOFTWARE YOU WILL NEED

The most important piece of software that you need is the adeno ITC, which is something that you're pretty familiar with. And I guess you already have it installed in the do not I.D.. We will need to install the DSP 32 Arduino core extension, which is something that I'm going to show you exactly how to do. Step by step apart from that, it's going to be good for you to have a text editor like Atom from Atom toward IO, a really nice text editor that we used to have a look at, especially at some of the files that come with their DSP 32 Arduino core extension. You're also going to need a terminal emulator tool like a serial tool for microwaves or real terms for Windows.

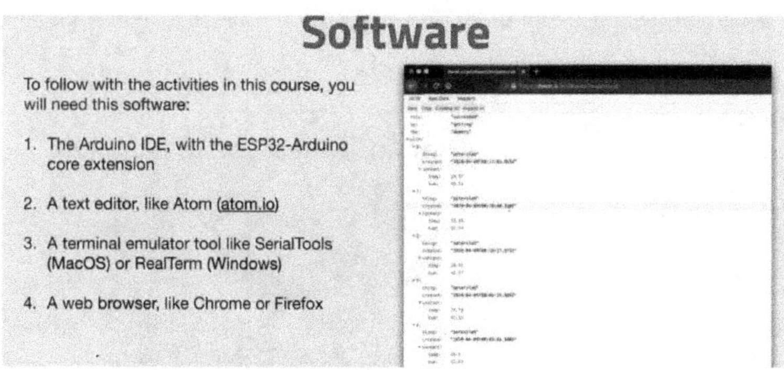

And we'll use this tool to play around with Bluetooth low energy later on. Of course, you are going to need a web browser like Chrome or Firefox in this image. Here I'm using Firefox to inspect the Jason file that comes back from one of the Internet of Things services that will be used when we demonstrate the Wi-Fi capability of the ISP 32. But that's about it. In summary, you need an idea on which will install the ESP32 Arduino extensions. A text editor to inspect text files and a terminal emulator in order to work with the Bluetooth example.

HARDWARE YOU WILL NEED

Of course, at the center of everything will be doing this project is to use P3 with the SPC to develop a kit version full board. The one that I'm using here and you see pictured here in this slide is the generic version of the SPC attitude kit V4 very common on eBay, on Amazon, pretty much anywhere else.

Hardware
To follow with the activities in this course, you will need this hardware (summary):
1. An ESP32 Dev kit v4 board
2. A couple of mini breadboards
3. Wires
4. Various components (detailed next)
Find this list at techexplorations.com/parts/esp32/

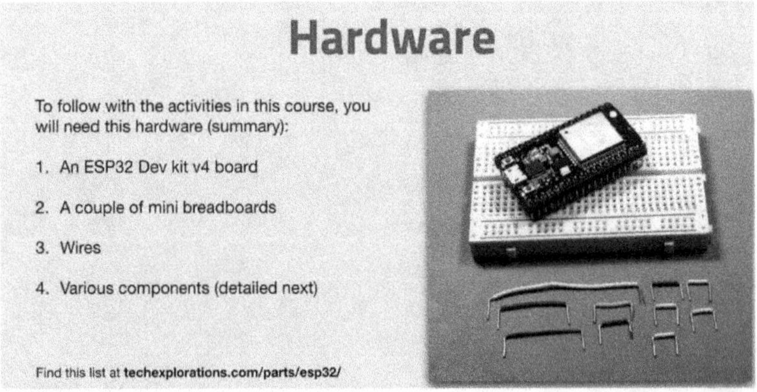

There are also a lot of very Asians on this board produced by various manufacturers that add hardware features on this base board, like, for example, circuit three for getting power from a lipo battery or charging a lithium battery and things of that sort. And those alternative boards may have differences in the way that they lay out, especially the way that the pins break out. So if you do use an alternative death kit, not the one pictured here, but something else from a different manufacturer, just be aware of those potential differences and you can still go ahead and use it with this project. As long as you understand what those differences are, especially the way that they pinch broken out and compensate for those in the sketch and in the way that the circuitry is laid out when you break. But. I also find it useful to have at least two of those boards on my desk at any time so that I can run simultaneous experiments. You can have, say, one board running my main experiment and then use my second use three to kit. Just to figure something out without having to dismantle my original circuit. So again, I do find that having two of those boards available really speeds up my rate of experimentation. Of course, then you're going to need a few mini ports. And I find that those mini breadboards, except for one experiment you'll see later with the seven seven displays, it's a little bit bigger in size with more wires. Find it for all of the experiments in this project, a mini breadboard which is actually perfect. Just a small amount of real estate with a small number of connections, makes things really clear, lowers the risk of mis-wiring and having problems of that sort. So I have a couple of those available then you're going to need wires to connect things together. Find those solid core wires again, like the ones pictured here are perfect for the needs of this project because they produce really clean and results in clean circuits. We can see exactly where wires go because they are right on the board without overhanging other components. So nice and clear, of course, around the HP 32, we're going to be using a variety of components that I'm going to detail next. And I should also mention that you can find the full list of these components with links to places like Amazon where you can purchase them from on my website at Tech explorations dot com for which like part four slash is P3 too. So let's check out the details. Of course we'll be playing around with any easy going that needs at least one read.

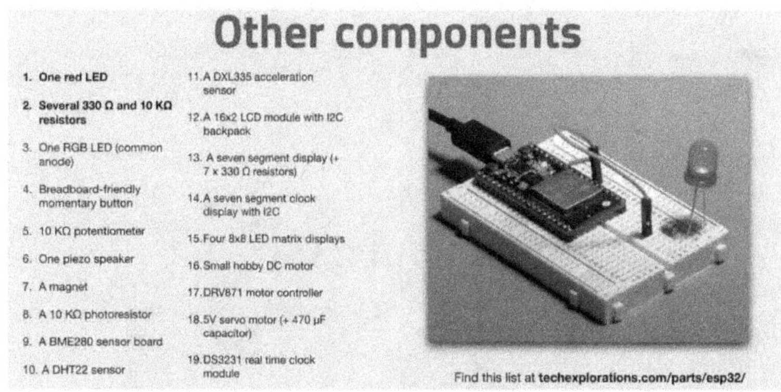
Other components
1. One red LED
2. Several 330 Ω and 10 KΩ resistors
3. One RGB LED (common anode)
4. Breadboard-friendly momentary button
5. 10 KΩ potentiometer
6. One piezo speaker
7. A magnet
8. A 10 KΩ photoresistor
9. A BME280 sensor board
10. A DHT22 sensor
11. A DXL335 acceleration sensor
12. A 16x2 LCD module with I2C backpack
13. A seven segment display (+ 7 x 330 Ω resistors)
14. A seven segment clock display with I2C
15. Four 8x8 LED matrix displays
16. Small hobby DC motor
17. DRV871 motor controller
18. 5V servo motor (+ 470 μF capacitor)
19. DS3231 real time clock module
Find this list at techexplorations.com/parts/esp32/

I recommend you buy a bunch and with the LTE you also need the same number of 330 ohm current limiting resistors. I've also listed a ten kiloton resistor here to use with the fourth resistor, which is down at number eight in the list. And also it's a pull up resistor for the DHT 22 sensor, which is down at number ten in this list. We are also going to experiment with LEDs. And with those you also need the 330 ohm current limiting resistors for each one of the colors on the LCD. I'm going to need a break board friendly, momentary button, and this button shows you how to configure it with an external pull up or pull down pain killer on the resistor, but also how to utilize the ESP three to the internal pullup resistor. You need a pendulum potentiometer to play around with the SB three to use analog inputs and a piezo speaker to make a little bit of noise. Yeah, that will do that when we are working out with the DC, the digital analog converter and we'll be listening to waveforms coming out of the converter.

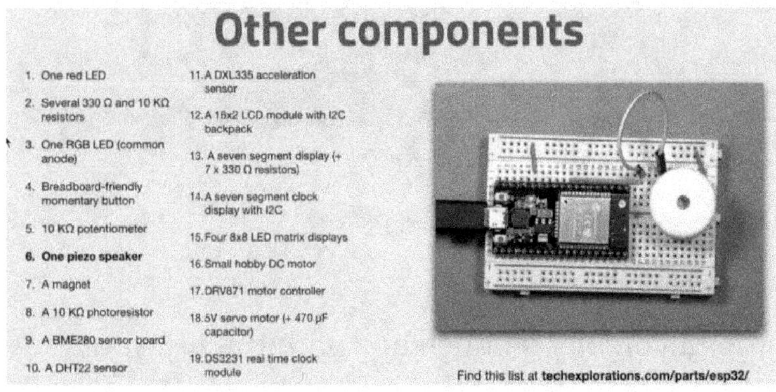
Other components
1. One red LED
2. Several 330 Ω and 10 KΩ resistors
3. One RGB LED (common anode)
4. Breadboard-friendly momentary button
5. 10 KΩ potentiometer
6. One piezo speaker
7. A magnet
8. A 10 KΩ photoresistor
9. A BME280 sensor board
10. A DHT22 sensor
11. A DXL335 acceleration sensor
12. A 16x2 LCD module with I2C backpack
13. A seven segment display (+ 7 x 330 Ω resistors)
14. A seven segment clock display with I2C
15. Four 8x8 LED matrix displays
16. Small hobby DC motor
17. DRV871 motor controller
18. 5V servo motor (+ 470 μF capacitor)
19. DS3231 real time clock module
Find this list at techexplorations.com/parts/esp32/

I will use a magnet to test one of the internal sensors in the ESP 32, then will need a ten kiloton for the resistor with its matching ten kilo on fixed resistor to measure light a BME 280 sensor board will be using that quite a lot to build environment sensing applications and little experiments. And we also need a DHT 22 sensor with its ten kiloton pull up resistor and will use a mixture of 335 analog acceleration since a 16 by two LCD module with the eyes could see backpack and will be using this screen quite a lot in a variety of experiments to display results and display text from various sensors or perish operations they can place on the ESP 32. We also need a seven segment display. This is a display that contains multiple entities and each of those entities requires its own 330 ohm current limiting resistance. As you can see here, I've placed this circuit on a larger breadboard, but in your case, if you don't have a larger breadboard, you can just use two of the mini breadboards together to accommodate this circuit and make it clean. We're also going to play around with a seven segment clock display with the ice switch see interface just to conserve in the number of ways that we need be using this display in experiment with the real time clock module that you can see here in the list in number 19, we'll do some experiments with eight by eight LCD matrix displays so you can get at least one of those. But if you have four, then we'll be able to plug them all together and create a larger display that will play with motors. So here I've got a small five volt hoby DC motor with the RV 871 motor controller, just as an experiment of what we can do with motors in the ESP 32. And I'm also going to do an experiment using a fire fold to serve a motor. And here it is pictured with a 470 micro rod capacitor which may or may not be needed depending on the size of the Miller. The motor that I've got in the picture here is tiny, so it had no problem getting power from the HP 32.

Other components

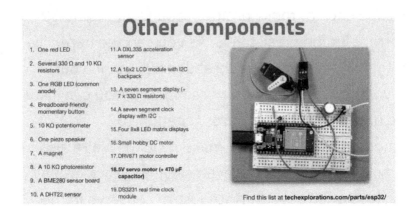

1. One red LED
2. Several 330 Ω and 10 KΩ resistors
3. One RGB LED (common anode)
4. Breadboard-friendly momentary button
5. 10 KΩ potentiometer
6. One piezo speaker
7. A magnet
8. A 10 KΩ photoresistor
9. A BME280 sensor board
10. A DHT22 sensor
11. A DXL335 acceleration sensor
12. A 16x2 LCD module with I2C backpack
13. A seven segment display (+ 7 x 330 Ω resistors)
14. A seven segment clock display with I2C
15. Four 8x8 LED matrix displays
16. Small hobby DC motor
17. DRV871 motor controller
18. **5V servo motor (+ 470 μF capacitor)**
19. DS3231 real time clock module

Find this list at **techexplorations.com/parts/esp32/**

But if you happen to use something bigger, then make sure that you have this capacitor up there as well on the power rail. And finally, we'll be playing around with time and data. So we need a 3 to 3 one real time clock module for that. So that wraps up the list of components that we need for this project. If we don't have all of those components, it's okay. You can still follow the course, but of course at some point you may want to do the experiments yourself so you can get them when needed. Don't go away yet. Check out the next project. It's a very important project because in that I am going to talk about the prerequisites of this project, the things that you need to know to be familiar with before you head to explore the rest of the projects further down. So very important. I'm also going to give you some advice on how to get the most out of the course and talk a little bit about the course structure so that you know what to expect.

Let's take a look at the required hardware for this project. Of course, at the center of everything will be doing this project is to use P3 with the SPC to develop a kit version full board. The one that I'm using here and you see pictured here in this slide is the generic version of the SPC attitude kit V4 very common on eBay, on Amazon, pretty much anywhere else.

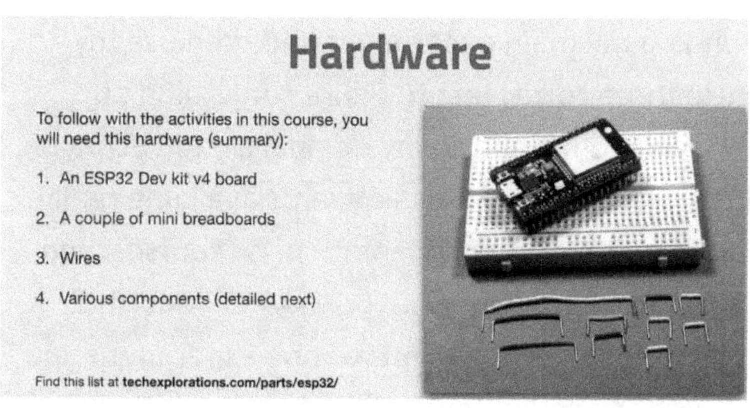
Hardware
To follow with the activities in this course, you will need this hardware (summary):
1. An ESP32 Dev kit v4 board
2. A couple of mini breadboards
3. Wires
4. Various components (detailed next)
Find this list at techexplorations.com/parts/esp32/

There are also a lot of very Asians on this board produced by various manufacturers that add hardware features on this base board, like, for example, circuit three for getting power from a lipo battery or charging a lithium battery and things of that sort. And those alternative boards may have differences in the way that they lay out, especially the way that the pins break out. So if you do use an alternative death kit, not the one pictured here, but something else from a different manufacturer, just be aware of those potential differences and you can still go ahead and use it with this project. As long as you understand what those differences are, especially the way that they pinch broken out and compensate for those in the sketch and in the way that the circuitry is laid out when you break. But. I also find it useful to have at least two of those boards on my desk at any time so that I can run simultaneous experiments. You can have, say, one board running my main experiment and then use my second use three to kit. Just to figure something out without having to dismantle my original circuit. So again, I do find that having two of those boards available really speeds up my rate of experimentation. Of course, then you're going to need a few mini ports. And I find that those mini breadboards, except for one experiment you'll see later with the seven seven displays, it's a little bit bigger in size with more wires. Find it for all of the experiments in this project, a mini breadboard which is actually perfect. Just a small amount of real estate with a small number of connections, makes things really clear, lowers the risk of mis-wiring and having problems of that sort. So I have a couple of those available then you're going to need wires to connect things together. Find those solid core wires again, like the ones pictured here are perfect for the needs of this project because they produce really clean and results in clean circuits. We can see exactly where wires go because they are right on the board without overhanging other components. So nice and clear, of course, around the HP 32, we're going to be using a variety of components that I'm going to detail next. And I should also mention that you can find the full list of these components with links to places like Amazon where you can purchase them from on my website at Tech explorations dot com for which like part four slash is P3 too. So let's check out the details. Of course we'll be playing around with any easy going that needs at least one read.

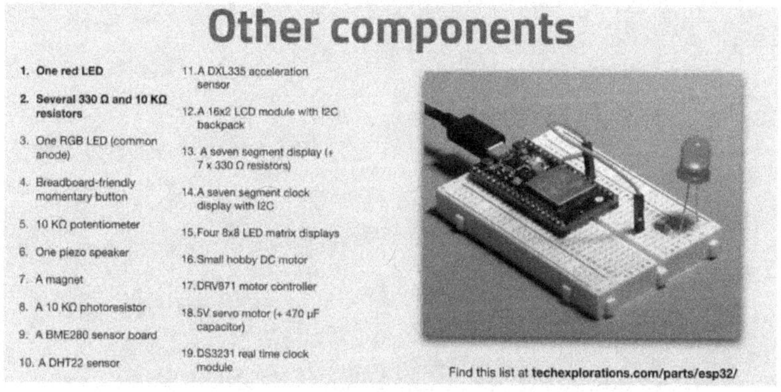
Other components
1. One red LED
2. Several 330 Ω and 10 KΩ resistors
3. One RGB LED (common anode)
4. Breadboard-friendly momentary button
5. 10 KΩ potentiometer
6. One piezo speaker
7. A magnet
8. A 10 KΩ photoresistor
9. A BME280 sensor board
10. A DHT22 sensor
11. A DXL335 acceleration sensor
12. A 16x2 LCD module with I2C backpack
13. A seven segment display (+ 7 x 330 Ω resistors)
14. A seven segment clock display with I2C
15. Four 8x8 LED matrix displays
16. Small hobby DC motor
17. DRV871 motor controller
18. 5V servo motor (+ 470 µF capacitor)
19. DS3231 real time clock module
Find this list at techexplorations.com/parts/esp32/

I recommend you buy a bunch and with the LTE you also need the same number of 330 ohm current limiting resistors. I've also listed a ten kiloton resistor here to use with the fourth resistor, which is down at number eight in the list. And also it's a pull up resistor for the DHT 22

sensor, which is down at number ten in this list. We are also going to experiment with LEDs. And with those you also need the 330 ohm current limiting resistors for each one of the colors on the LCD. I'm going to need a break board friendly, momentary button, and this button shows you how to configure it with an external pull up or pull down pain killer on the resistor, but also how to utilize the ESP three to the internal pullup resistor. You need a pendulum potentiometer to play around with the SB three to use analog inputs and a piezo speaker to make a little bit of noise. Yeah, that will do that when we are working out with the DC, the digital analog converter and we'll be listening to waveforms coming out of the converter.

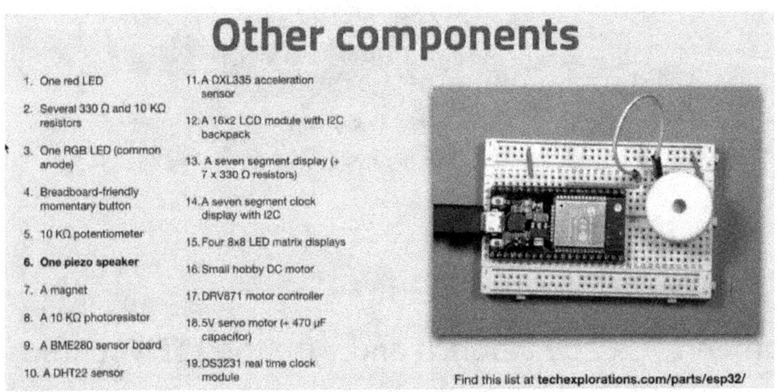

Other components
1. One red LED
2. Several 330 Ω and 10 KΩ resistors
3. One RGB LED (common anode)
4. Breadboard-friendly momentary button
5. 10 KΩ potentiometer
6. One piezo speaker
7. A magnet
8. A 10 KΩ photoresistor
9. A BME280 sensor board
10. A DHT22 sensor
11. A DXL335 acceleration sensor
12. A 16x2 LCD module with I2C backpack
13. A seven segment display (+ 7 x 330 Ω resistors)
14. A seven segment clock display with I2C
15. Four 8x8 LED matrix displays
16. Small hobby DC motor
17. DRV871 motor controller
18. 5V servo motor (+ 470 μF capacitor)
19. DS3231 real time clock module
Find this list at techexplorations.com/parts/esp32/

I will use a magnet to test one of the internal sensors in the ESP 32, then will need a ten kiloton for the resistor with its matching ten kilo on fixed resistor to measure light a BME 280 sensor board will be using that quite a lot to build environment sensing applications and little experiments. And we also need a DHT 22 sensor with its ten kiloton pull up resistor and will use a mixture of 335 analog acceleration since a 16 by two LCD module with the eyes could see backpack and will be using this screen quite a lot in a variety of experiments to display results and display text from various sensors or perish operations they can place on the ESP 32. We also need a seven segment display. This is a display that contains multiple entities and each of those entities requires its own 330 ohm current limiting resistance. As you can see here, I've placed this circuit on a larger breadboard, but in your case, if you don't have a larger breadboard, you can just use two of the mini breadboards together to accommodate this circuit and make it clean. We're also going to play around with a seven segment clock display with the ice switch see interface just to conserve in the number of ways that we need be using this display in experiment with the real time clock module that you can see here in the list in number 19, we'll do some experiments with eight by eight LCD matrix displays so you can get at least one of those. But if you have four, then we'll be able to plug them all together and create a larger display that will play with motors. So here I've got a small five volt hoby DC motor with the RV 871 motor controller, just as an experiment of what we can do with motors in the ESP 32. And I'm also going to do an experiment using a fire fold to serve a motor. And here it is pictured with a 470 micro rod capacitor which may or may not be needed depending on the size of the Miller. The motor that I've got in the picture here is tiny, so it had no problem getting power from the HP 32.

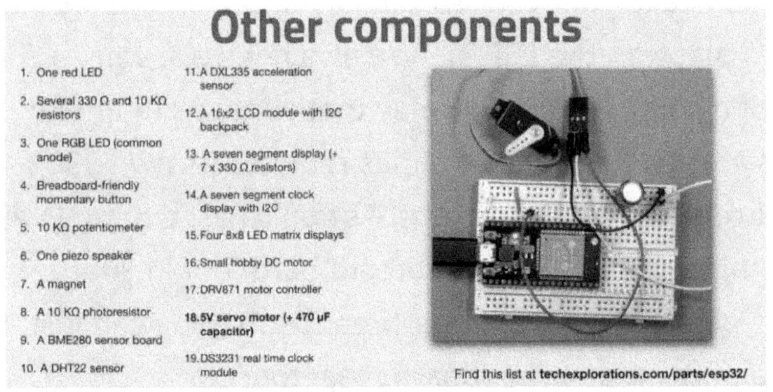
Other components
1. One red LED
2. Several 330 Ω and 10 KΩ resistors
3. One RGB LED (common anode)
4. Breadboard-friendly momentary button
5. 10 KΩ potentiometer
6. One piezo speaker
7. A magnet
8. A 10 KΩ photoresistor
9. A BME280 sensor board
10. A DHT22 sensor
11. A DXL335 acceleration sensor
12. A 16x2 LCD module with I2C backpack
13. A seven segment display (+ 7 x 330 Ω resistors)
14. A seven segment clock display with I2C
15. Four 8x8 LED matrix displays
16. Small hobby DC motor
17. DRV871 motor controller
18. 5V servo motor (+ 470 μF capacitor)
19. DS3231 real time clock module
Find this list at techexplorations.com/parts/esp32/

But if you happen to use something bigger, then make sure that you have this capacitor up there as well on the power rail. And finally, we'll be playing around with time and data. So we need a 3 to 3 one real time clock module for that. So that wraps up the list of components that we need for this project. If we don't have all of those components, it's okay. You can still follow the course, but of course at some point you may want to do the experiments yourself so you can get them when needed. Don't go away yet. Check out the next project. It's a very important project because in that I am going to talk about the prerequisites of this project, the things that you need to know to be familiar with before you head to explore the rest of the projects further down. So very important. I'm also going to give you some advice on how to get the most out of the course and talk a little bit about the course structure so that you know what to expect.

HOW TO GET THE MOST OUT

because in this project I'm going to talk about prerequisites, how to make the most out of this project, and give you an outlook of the structure of the course. Let's get started. So the prerequisites, the most important thing here is that you must be familiar with the know. You must have already done a little bit of work with it and be comfortable with the Adreno as a device in the hardware, with creating circuits around the arduino and with programming it using the adreno i.t. If you are a recent graduate or are doing a step by step getting started and perhaps you are now going through doing a step by step getting serious, then you are at the perfect stage of your development to get into the SB 32. But if you don't have any experience with the Arduino, then really think carefully. If you want to continue this project, you are going to find it a bit overwhelming. In my opinion, the SB three two is not a good first board for anyone. I do not, you know, in my opinion, again, is the perfect way to begin your education in microcontrollers and programming. SB 32 is a very powerful board that can be very overwhelming for beginners, and that's why I'm asking you to be careful here and not to get into this project unless you have some familiarity with it.

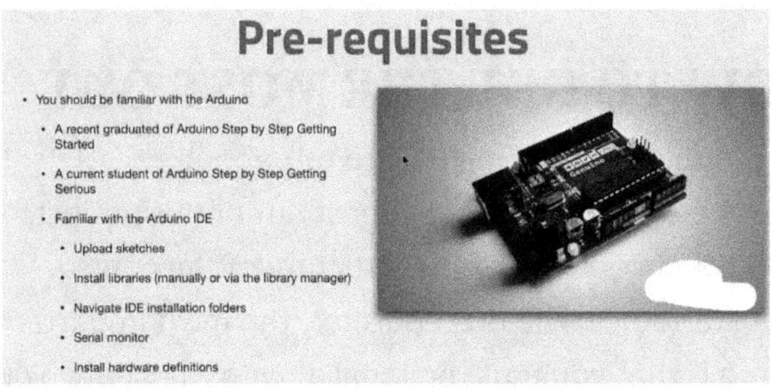

Do you know? So you need to be familiar with the adeno idea. You need to be able to, for example, upload sketches and install libraries both manually or via the library manager and to navigate the integrated development environment installation. For this, you should also be able to do a bit of programming. Again, you don't need to be an expert programing in adreno. I'm not an expert at programming myself, but you do need to be comfortable with the language. So for example, you should be able to look at the code example that I've got here, which is from one of my helium examples. I do know step by step, getting serious and understanding, at least in general, what is happening here. You should also be able to write your own simple sketches, either outright or by modifying existing examples or third party sketches. But to be able to get those sketches to do what you want them to do. So if you are able to do all that, if you are comfortable with the idea and you are able to write simple programs or modify existing product programs and understand what you see when you see a relatively simple idea in a program, then you go to continue. Another thing that will be doing a lot here in this project is to look at documentation, especially if the limitation that looks like this and this documentation gives us a lot of insight on what is going on with the hardware of the SB 42 and with its API with this programming interface. So I'll be digging into this limitation quite a lot and it's important for you to not be afraid of it, to be comfortable at looking at documentation, even if you don't understand everything in it. It's true that this documentation can get really deep into various issues that may not make much sense, but I promise you that you will always learn something new no matter which page in the documentation you look at. So I ask you to not be afraid when you look at the limitation and just to persevere with it. And you'll be learning a lot. Also, another thing to remember is that I'm going to talk about the philosophy of this project later. I'm not explaining everything in great detail, but I am providing a lot of leads, a lot of points to documentation that you can look at to make the most out of this project. You need to be comfortable with following those leads and even discovering your own leads as you are researching a topic. A feature of this project is the code repository. So the course repository is on GitHub and you can see it's your role here and it contains all of the sketches that I'll be demonstrating in this project as well as the schematics. And you can see examples of those here as well.

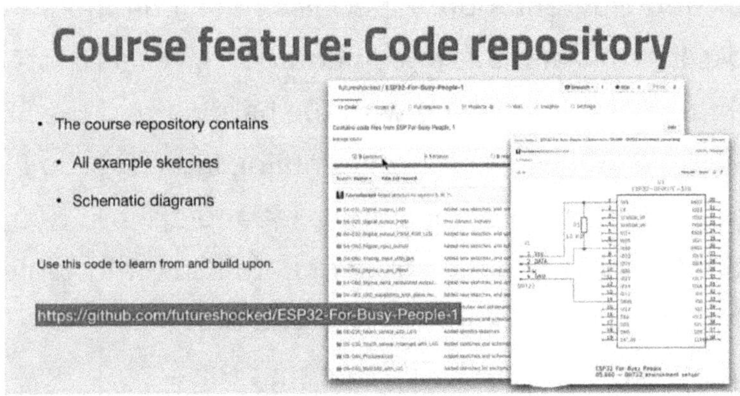

So you can always match a project with its example sketch and the schematic by looking at the number of the project. So he can see, for example, in this view of the

GitHub repository, every 4-- with the number zero four -0 four row. So that is the number of the project that you want to look for in the curriculum and then match it with the code and schematic files in the GitHub repository. To put this, you are really on a shortcut in your browser so that it is always easy to get to and to access. If you have enrolled to this project on the explorations website, then you also know that there is a dedicated discussion forum. This is where you can go and ask more general questions about your projects, for example, or asking for advice from others. And this is where the ESP 3 to 4 busy people, students and instructors like myself will be checking out frequently. A quick look at the course strategy.

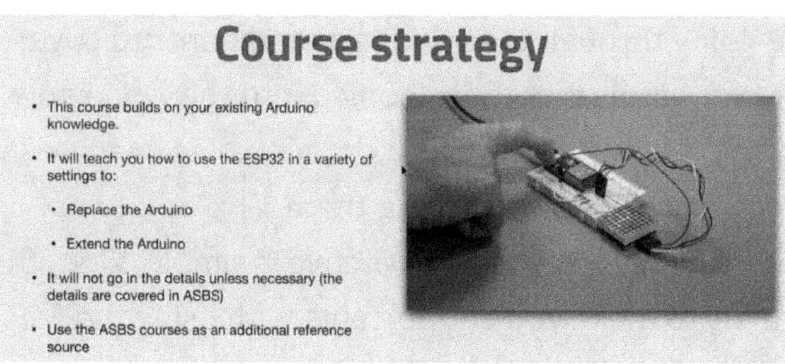

Course strategy
This course builds on your existing Arduino knowledge.
It will teach you how to use the ESP32 in a variety of settings to:
Replace the Arduino
Extend the Arduino
It will not go in the details unless necessary (the details are covered in ASBS)
Use the ASBS courses as an additional reference source

Since I started designing this project, I wanted to create a course that builds on your existing Arduino knowledge. I didn't want to scrap that knowledge and start from scratch because we have all invested quite a lot in learning the Arduino. So this project builds on your existing Arduino knowledge, and that's why this idea of knowledge is a core prerequisite of this project. What this project will do, though, is to extend this knowledge and it will teach you how to use the ESP 52 in a variety of settings, which means never writing of circuits, for example, components and so on different contexts in order to both replace and extend the. I do know because it is more capable. At the very least you can use it to replace your Arduino with this board. But you will also learn how to take advantage of its additional resources memory, for example, speed and pains and so on in order to extend your Arduino. As I said earlier, this project builds on existing knowledge and it will not go into details as some going through the various experiments to cover content that has already been copied into the, you know, step by step courses. So for such details, you can always go back to those courses and use them. This additional reference source. The course objective is simple. First, the course aims to make you comfortable with using the ESP 32 as an alternative to you are doing it in all of your projects and from that point on which to make you self-sufficient in extending your skill and knowledge. The course covers a few important topics in the world of the SB 32, but definitely not all of them, and it's so much more that you can learn. And one of the objectives here is to make you capable of going out and explore more on your own. And we thought that said, let's check out the course structure, what's included. You see that? I've got the various sections listed here from 1 to 11.

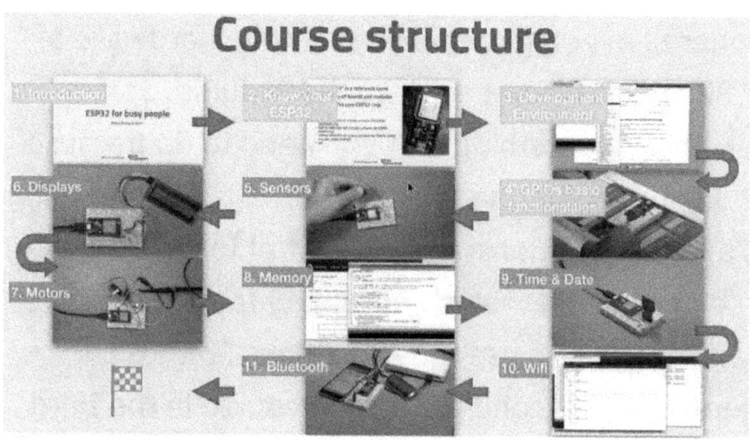

The first four sections have got green labels, which means that do not miss those projects. You must follow them serially one after the other and make sure you do them before you go into the rest. The blue labels indicate sections that you can access out of order if you wish. Of course you can go from cover to cover, but if you are working, for example, right now on a project that requires you to work with time and date, then after you complete the first four sections, you can just jump straight into section number nine and and have a look at the time and date and how to use a real time clock in your project with the ESP three to. But if you don't have a particular project that you're working on, just take these sections one at a time and your learning will be solid. So the introduction is what we're doing right now is actually going through the last project of the introductory section, and that will be followed by the second section. Know your use at 32. That's where I'm going to drill down to the hardware of the ESP 32 and also compare it to the Arduino. So definitely this is something that you need to do because the ESP 32, just like in the modern world, is not one thing. There's a lot of variations, there's a lot of features that need to be explained that it's necessary to do before we actually go ahead and use those systems. So those subsystems in the second part of the course in the third section, I'm going to show you how to set up your development environment. As you know, I will be using the old idea. But we do need to install the support for the esthetic too, and I'll show you how to do that in Section three in Windows and Mac OS. Then we'll go into the first actual experimental section, Section four, where we'll drill into the GPOs and show you how to get basic functionality out of those areas. And that's where we play with these. For example, in section five, we'll work with Sensis. I'll show you how to use some of the built-in sensors in the ESP 32 and how to attach external sensors, readings. Then we'll go to Section six, we'll play around with displays. There's of course, the ubiquitous LCD display, but we also have clock displays, seven segment displays and eight by eight metrics displays and displays are an important part of the user interface in any project. So definitely worth going through this one. Then we'll look at how to create movement and the way by which motor control works in the HP three two is very, very similar to how you do this in the adreno. So in section seven, I want to show you some basic examples showing how to use DC Motors and two servo motors. And here definitely you can use your I do know knowledge to use all sorts of motors which will be one of the really nice features of the ESP 32 the abundance of memory both RAM and also non volatile flash memory that is available. And in Section eight, I'll show you how to use the memory resources that come with these P3 to in Section nine. I'll show you how to use an external real time clock in order to help your HP three to tell time and date and the real time clock that I'll be using also has some interesting features that we will be exploiting in order to make better use of the DSP three two hardware namely will be using interrupts that are generated by the external time and date module. The last two sections are about wireless communications. The really cool feature about the HP 32 is that it has support for both Wi-Fi and Bluetooth classic and really this low energy and starting with section ten will work first to learn the Wi-Fi module. So we'll go through a series of mini projects to learn how to use the Wi-Fi module on the HP three two to communicate with the Internet. And here I'll show you how to send graphics samples to Internet of Things services and produce dashboards where you can display data coming from sensors and even how to create a simple web server running on your HP 32 quite fast and powerful. That is as well thanks to the computational resources of the ISP. Three to and while Wi-Fi is great for internet communications and Internet of Things applications, if you want to communicate with the near field devices, so with your phone, for example, or with your heart rate monitor, then you need Bluetooth. And in the last section, section 11, I'll show you how to do that. So in section 11, I'll show you how to use Bluetooth low energy and the classic Bluetooth so that you can use your ESP 32in connection with another device as a serial device. And that's it. At that point, you have completed the course and I'm confident that you will have achieved objectives. So with all that said, let's begin with our first actual hands-on exploration of the ESP 32.

THE ESP32 MODULE

Let's begin this section with a close look at the ESP module that powers the development kit that will be used in this project. In this picture here, the ESP 32 module is indicated by the green box on the development kit, and it's got a name. It's called ESP Wroom 32. That's the particular model of the ESP 32 module that we are looking at. And as you see, there's more. So ESP 32 is P32 is a reference name. It's a bit like saying Arduino, and by saying Arduino we mean a variety of different boards, not just a single board. In particular, the ESP 32 is a reference name for the modules Variations of the device on this development kit that is enclosed inside the green rectangle, not the development kit itself, but the module. And that's a few different modules out there that respond to the same reference name. So for example, we've got the ESP 32 W room or bathroom. I'm not sure exactly how to pronounce that. It's room 32, which is the module that actually powers the development kit that I'll be using in this project. And this contains the SPF 30 2d0wd Q6 chip and more about this in a moment. This also the very another variant, the ESP 32 from 32 D, which contains a slightly different chip that powers it and the source of the rover modules such as the ESP 3 to 4 over IP, which also contains that ESP 30 2d0d chip, but with additional memory and many, many more.

The "ESP32" is a reference name to a variety of boards and modules based on the core ESP32 chip.

For example:

- ESP32-WROOM-32 module contains the ESP32-DOWDQ6 chip
- ESP32-WROOM-32D module contains the ESP32-DOWD chip
- ESP32-WROVER-IB module contains the ESP32-DOWD but with added PSRAM
- etc.

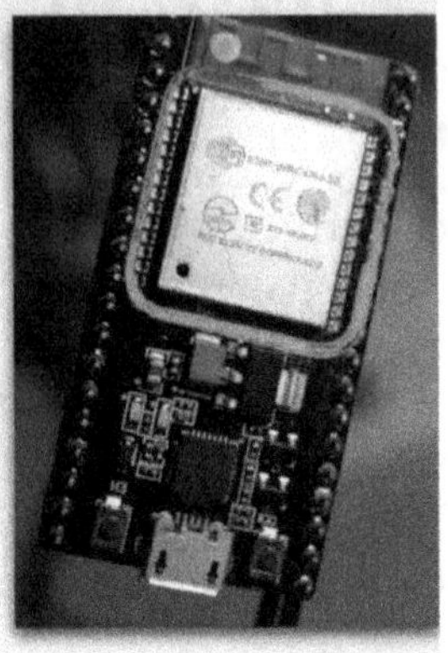

Each of those modules and chip combinations has its own characteristics and it's optimized for a particular purpose. So typically the variation has to do with how much memory is present, whether or not there is pseudo static ram, the kind of antenna that they use, or whether they use a single or a dual core processor and so on. And down the bottom of this slide, of course, further reading, if you're interested to know more, for example, about what sort of static RAM is and information about antennas and so on, you can find the module in the development kit that I'll be using in this project has got a chip with a D in its name, which denotes dual core, and it's this one here, the ESP32 through 32.

The "ESP32" is a reference name to a variety of boards and modules based on the core ESP32 chip.

Each module and chip combination has a unique set of characteristics.

- Amount of flash memory (typically 4MB)
- Presence and amount of PSRAM (pseudo-static RAM[1])
  - 8 MB Available in WROVER modules
- Type of antenna
  - MIFA: Meandered Inverted-F Antenna[2]
  - U.FL: antenna connector for an external antenna
- Number of processing cores
  - Chips with "D" after "ESP32" denote dual core
  - Chips with "S" after "ESP32" denote single core

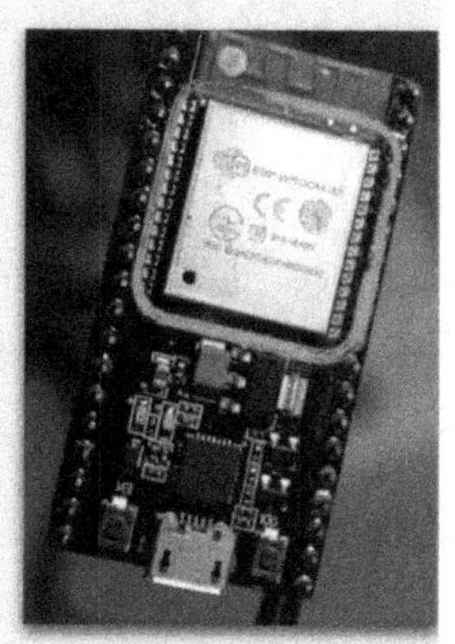

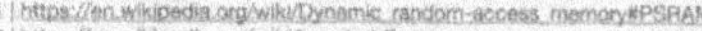

1 | https://en.wikipedia.org/wiki/Dynamic_random-access_memory#PSRAM
2 | https://en.wikipedia.org/wiki/Inverted-F_antenna
3 | https://docs.espressif.com/projects/esp-idf/en/latest/hw-reference/modules-and-boards.html#wroom-solo-and-wrover-modules

It contains the ISP 30 2d0wd. This d stands for dual core Q six chip. It's got four megabytes. So flash memory or I'll be showing you how to use that flash memory to store data. It has no static ram, no pseudo static ram, if you'd say, and a misfire antenna my f a which stands for me under inverted F antenna, you can see the antenna up at the top edge of the board with its zigzag pattern. This antenna is a good fit for the ESP32 because of the small amount of available board space allocated to the antenna. We want this antenna to be etched on the PC itself instead of needing an external component for the antenna. And because there's not much space on the board, you can see this very little amount of space available. And if the antenna uses a meander shape so that we end up with a full electrical length antenna that fits this small available space, Another variant of the ISP 3 to 4 room are the 32 D and 32 new variants. So these contain the ISP 30 2d0d chip. Still, I've got a four megabyte flash and no static ram and they're D model still has a meter antenna, but the new model has a connector that allows us to connect an external antenna. In addition, both of those variants are smaller than the one that will be using this project. Then the ISP said to room 32 in the ISP three to get version four, which are used in the June 2022 update of this project you'll find the ESP32 wroom 32 E module. There is also a version of the Vision for Deaf kit with the 30 2ue variant of the module which contains a connector for an external antenna.

ESP32-WROOM-32E
ESP32-WROOM-32UE

- Contains the **ESP32-D0WD-V3** chip, offering higher stability and safety performance compared to the ESP32-WROOM-32
- **4 MB Flash** (some variants go up to 16MB)
- No PSRAM
- **MIFA** antenna for the "E" model
- **U.FL** antenna connector for the "UE" model
- This is the module used in the official dev kit version 4.
- See https://espressif.com/en/products/modules for a listing of all current module models.

This module contains the ISP 3 to 0 WD vision three chip and is an updated version of the original ISP three to Room 32 module. It offers higher stability and better safety performance compared to the original. The 32 E has the same amount of flash options and no RAM. The updated version is slightly more expensive than the original, though in my latest market research I was able to find ESP three two decades with both versions of the module that is both the ESP three, Tube Room 32 and the ISP 32, Room 32. E if you can find the 32 E variant, then you should go for it. But if you can't rest assured that the basic Room 32 will allow you to get through the course without any issues. The VO5 variant is also a more powerful variant compared to the room models. I'm not going to go through the details here, but from this summary you can see that even though they have the same amount of flash as stained room modules, they contain a spy shooter, a static ram. While the very models have got none of that, you can still get them with an integrated antenna or an external useful antenna. And the heif variants that can operate with as low as 1.8 volts and up to 144 megahertz of clock speed. I really like the schematic of the ISP 30 2dw dq6 module which powers my ESP32 development kit because it provides a map of all the hardware that is embedded in this microcontroller.

ESP32-WROVER

More powerful compared to the WROOM models

- **ESP32-WROVER** and **ESP32-WROVER-I** use the **ESP32-D0WDQ6** chip (same as ESP32-WROOM-32)
- **ESP32-WROVER-B** and **ESP32-WROVER-IB** use the **ESP32-D0WD** chip (same as ESP32-WROOM-32D and U)
- **4 MB Flash** (similar to WROOM modules)
- **8 MB SPI PSRAM** (WROOM have none)
- **MIFA** or **U.FL** antenna
- Depending on the model, can operate at **1.8V**, and up to **144MHz** clock speed

So this is a summary of its capabilities. In a sense, at the center you can see the core in the memory. There's one or two x ten star L six microprocessors here, depending on the module that you're using. The one that I'll be using contains a dual core processor with its own ROM and static ram. At the top left of this diagram, you can see the radio hardware, including the Wi-Fi and Bluetooth. And on the right side there's the embedded flash memory we're using to store our programs and other data and files for our various experiments. The peripheral interfaces I squid see and I spy this cryptography as well available so that we can use TLC and SSL encryption when we are communicating with the Internet. And this also low power management subsystem down the bottom left of this diagram. It's a great summary of the hardware architecture of the SB 32. And to wrap it up is a slide that contains the SB three two module common features we haven't discussed yet the development kit as a whole, but if you focus on the SB 32 module, here's some of the highlights. So one or two courses for the processor, there's plenty of internal memory ability to connect external RAM. It's a bunch of tiny missing watch watchdogs that will be using this project. These are radio interfaces, lots of bios and so on. He can take a time to walk yourself through this list now that we have a better understanding of what lies in the center of our development kit, where the DSP 32 module sits, let's have a look at the hardware around that. The hardware that is contained in the SB 32 development kit is what exposes all this functionality to us so that we can play around with it. So let's move on to the next project and have a look at the iOS P32 development kit.

ESP32 VS ARDUINO

In this project, we'll have a look at the differences and similarities between the ESP 32 and the R2, and in particular, they're doing it. We know that most of us are familiar with. These two are totally different. I'm not sure if you've guessed it, but not only do they look different, but they're architecture is also totally different. So we've got a different hardware architecture. The built in capabilities are all different. The amount of memory that they enclose, the processing capabilities in power, the number of GPO sets, they expose the communications features and more and more all of those things are really different between these two microcontrollers.

The closest Arduino boards that I can find to the ESP 32 are probably the Adreno 1 to 1 or the Arduino zero at least, and those share some of the features that the ESP 32has such as integrated Wi-Fi and Bluetooth and the computational capacity. But even there, the differences are more than the similarities. What makes the ESP 32a very good choice for people that are familiar with their do not eat this software expressive, which is the company that designs and makes the ISP 32, has made a huge effort in writing software that bridges the hardware gap between the ESP 32 and the ADRENO thanks to the software that we call. As you'll see later, the HP 32. I do not score. We can use the ESP 32 as if we are using the adreno Again, you see that in practice very soon. So thanks again to the software. The ESP 32 can be treated as being compatible with the ADRENO. We can use the ADRENO. It is a developing environment. We can use a programming language that matches almost one on one with the language that we have learned for the adreno. And to a large extent we can reuse almost 90% of the adreno libraries in software that we write for the P3 two, which is pretty amazing. As I have said again, when you consider the differences in the hardware architecture between these two, the HP 32 works with the rDNA I.D., with the installation of the HP 32 Arduino core and the integration between these two is remarkable. Once you install the ESP32 Arduino core, you get access to a large variety of development kits that are based on the ESP 32 and you should get a load of example sketches and you can essentially start using it right away. Even when it comes to the libraries.

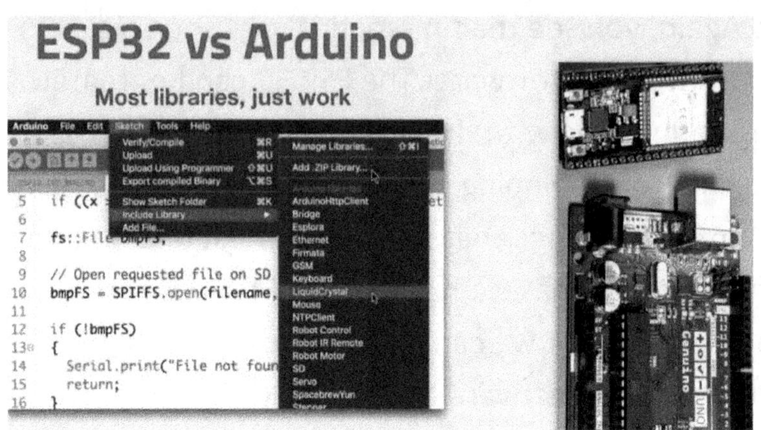

Most of the Arduino libraries will just work with the HP 32 again because of the ESP32 Arduino core software that this person has developed. Of course, the ESP32 contains unique features that are not present in the adreno and to take advantage of those features such as the SBI filesystem here that I've got projects about in this project in order to take advantage of this feature, just press F ahead to provide compatible libraries that we can use via the Arduino idea. So again, no problem here. So who is the ISP? 3 to 4? Well, it's definitely not for beginners. I've said this before, if you're not familiar with the Adreno, then the ESP32 will be complex, will be a difficult thing to learn and I don't recommend it. I think that the Arduino is a much better choice for you makers. It's a simpler device, it's simpler to program, it's more forgiving as well to problems in wiring and to mistakes in wiring is more robust, so it's easier to set up. But of course you can just download it, plug in your Arduino, and off you go. You don't have to make any modifications to it once you build up your knowledge and skill on the Arduino in particular, they are doing it, you know.

ESP32 vs Arduino

The ESP32 is perfect for Maker with at least intermediate Arduino skills.

- Any ESP32 capability that matches the Arduino, has no learning curve.
- Unique capabilities can be learned incrementally.
- You get Wifi, Bluetooth, lots of memory and speed for "free".
- You can treat the ESP32 as a supercharged Arduino Uno
- You can also grow your skills to a totally new class.
- You can finally move away from the Arduino IDE to a more complete IDE.

Then the ESP32 provides a perfect opportunity to extend and expand on those skills. The additional features that ESP32 contains means that you can do. We can work on more interesting projects and that alone is very desirable. So you can start working with HP 32 using your existing Arduino skills essentially. No, or very little learning curve. And then anything else that you want to do on top of what you already know means that you can improve your skills incrementally and gradually, gently, without much stress. You also get Wi-Fi and Bluetooth and lots of memory essentially for free. Here also denotes the monetary issue that the HP three dev kit is actually cheaper and Arduino, you know, you get more of these benefits for a lower price at that level you can treat the Speaker two as a super charged device that is doing its own thing faster and in many respects. And when you feel confident and ready, you can actually move away from the original idea to a more complete integrated development environment. And I'm going to show you how to do that in upcoming courses that I'm now working to produce. So with that said and done, let's dig into the next project where we'll discuss the ECP three to keep our interest.

GPIOS

In this project, we'll have a look at the bios and how we refer to them and the various functions that they express. And most of the 38 panes of the HP 32 module are broken now in two rows of pins in the IS P32 dev kit, but not all of them. So in particular here is the module, the ESP 32 broom module. It is this hardware device in the top end of the development kit and you can see how those pins come out of its three sides. When we put the development kit around the module, what we get is that we have several of the clamps of the module itself, but not all of them that are broken out along the two sides of the development kit. Those are marked at J2 on the left and J3 on the right.

In this diagram, you can find this table here in the original documentation of the S.P. 32 room, and I've got the air rail for that and at the bottom right side of this slide. But what I want to show you here is that each of these pins exposes more than one function. So these pins are all multifunction.

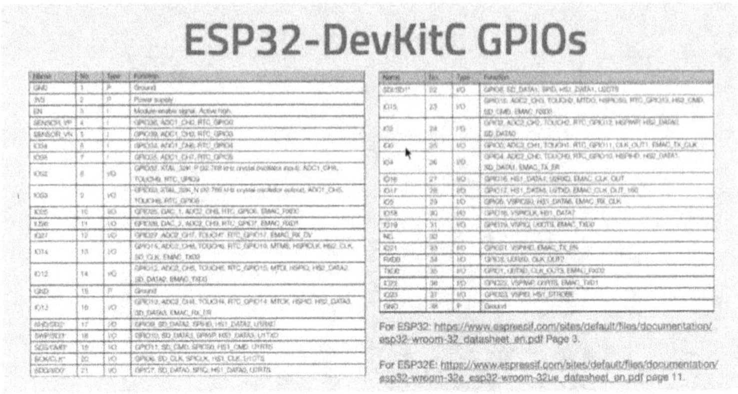

ESP32-DevKitC GPIOs

Name	No.	Type	Function
GND	1	P	Ground
3V3	2	P	Power supply
EN	3	I	Module-enable signal. Active high.
SENSOR_VP	4	I	GPIO36, ADC1_CH0, RTC_GPIO0
SENSOR_VN	5	I	GPIO39, ADC1_CH3, RTC_GPIO3
IO34	6	I	GPIO34, ADC1_CH6, RTC_GPIO4
IO35	7	I	GPIO35, ADC1_CH7, RTC_GPIO5
IO32	8	I/O	GPIO32, XTAL_32K_P (32.768 kHz crystal oscillator input), ADC1_CH4, TOUCH9, RTC_GPIO9
IO33	9	I/O	GPIO33, XTAL_32K_N (32.768 kHz crystal oscillator output), ADC1_CH5, TOUCH8, RTC_GPIO8
IO25	10	I/O	GPIO25, DAC_1, ADC2_CH8, RTC_GPIO6, EMAC_RXD0
IO26	11	I/O	GPIO26, DAC_2, ADC2_CH9, RTC_GPIO7, EMAC_RXD1
IO27	12	I/O	GPIO27, ADC2_CH7, TOUCH7, RTC_GPIO17, EMAC_RX_DV
IO14	13	I/O	GPIO14, ADC2_CH6, TOUCH6, RTC_GPIO16, MTMS, HSPICLK, HS2_CLK, SD_CLK, EMAC_TXD2
IO12	14	I/O	GPIO12, ADC2_CH5, TOUCH5, RTC_GPIO15, MTDI, HSPIQ, HS2_DATA2, SD_DATA2, EMAC_TXD3
GND	15	P	Ground
IO13	16	I/O	GPIO13, ADC2_CH4, TOUCH4, RTC_GPIO14, MTCK, HSPID, HS2_DATA3, SD_DATA3, EMAC_RX_ER
SHD/SD2*	17	I/O	GPIO9, SD_DATA2, SPIHD, HS1_DATA2, U1RXD
SWP/SD3*	18	I/O	GPIO10, SD_DATA3, SPIWP, HS1_DATA3, U1TXD
SCS/CMD*	19	I/O	GPIO11, SD_CMD, SPICS0, HS1_CMD, U1RTS
SCK/CLK*	20	I/O	GPIO6, SD_CLK, SPICLK, HS1_CLK, U1CTS
SDO/SD0*	21	I/O	GPIO7, SD_DATA0, SPIQ, HS1_DATA0, U2RTS
SDI/SD1*	22	I/O	GPIO8, SD_DATA1, SPID, HS1_DATA1, U2CTS
IO15	23	I/O	GPIO15, ADC2_CH3, TOUCH3, MTDO, HSPICS0, RTC_GPIO13, HS2_CMD, SD_CMD, EMAC_RXD3
IO2	24	I/O	GPIO2, ADC2_CH2, TOUCH2, RTC_GPIO12, HSPIWP, HS2_DATA0, SD_DATA0
IO0	25	I/O	GPIO0, ADC2_CH1, TOUCH1, RTC_GPIO11, CLK_OUT1, EMAC_TX_CLK
IO4	26	I/O	GPIO4, ADC2_CH0, TOUCH0, RTC_GPIO10, HSPIHD, HS2_DATA1, SD_DATA1, EMAC_TX_ER
IO16	27	I/O	GPIO16, HS1_DATA4, U2RXD, EMAC_CLK_OUT
IO17	28	I/O	GPIO17, HS1_DATA5, U2TXD, EMAC_CLK_OUT_180
IO5	29	I/O	GPIO5, VSPICS0, HS1_DATA6, EMAC_RX_CLK
IO18	30	I/O	GPIO18, VSPICLK, HS1_DATA7
IO19	31	I/O	GPIO19, VSPIQ, U0CTS, EMAC_TXD0
NC	32		
IO21	33	I/O	GPIO21, VSPIHD, EMAC_TX_EN
RXD0	34	I/O	GPIO3, U0RXD, CLK_OUT2
TXD0	35	I/O	GPIO1, U0TXD, CLK_OUT3, EMAC_RXD2
IO22	36	I/O	GPIO22, VSPIWP, U0RTS, EMAC_TXD1
IO23	37	I/O	GPIO23, VSPID, HS1_STROBE
GND	38	P	Ground

For ESP32: https://www.espressif.com/sites/default/files/documentation/esp32-wroom-32_datasheet_en.pdf Page 3.

For ESP32E: https://www.espressif.com/sites/default/files/documentation/esp32-wroom-32e_esp32-wroom-32ue_datasheet_en.pdf page 11.

So, for example, you can look here, go get the name column. Let's pick GPIO 34 So GPIO 34 is a physical pin six. It's an input and it exposes these functions. So it's a GPO, It's also one of the analog to digital converter channels and also connects to the RTC GPIO for let's pick up another one here is Pro two, which is physical PIN 24 and this is an input output pane and has got all of these functionalities in apart from just being a chip area too. It's also an analog to digital converter on PIN Channel two. It also exposes a touch sensor and it is a part of the SPI hardware and so on. So I've printed this out and I keep it close by when I'm working with CSP three to sort of quickly make reference and figure out what functionalities are available for any given pin. So here's another example of TPR or 15, which is a physical pin. 23 is input and output type pin and exposes all of these functionalities. Just be aware that pros 6 to 11 are connected to the motion's integrated SPI flash and can be used for external connections. So these are not broken out in the development kit. I've also developed this map that you can download and print out and keep handy when you're working with HP 3 to 3 out of this project and I'll be making frequent reference to this map instead of using the more elaborate table of pins and pin functions that I showed you earlier, I've written down the most commonly used functions for all of the pins of the development kit.

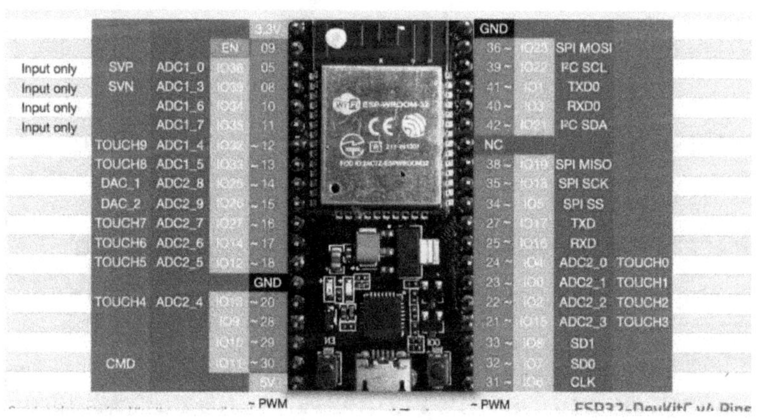

So for example, here I can see that GPIO 32, which is physical PIN 12 in the ISP module, gives me access to one of the touch sensors and to the analog to digital converter. And these are the functions that are typically used most often. I'm also going to be making reference to

PINS based on their GPIO number. So based on the yellow numbers here, no to the physical pins. So beware of that in most cases, unless otherwise noted, I'll be making reference to pins based on their GPIO number instead of the physical pin numbers. Another feature of this map is this tilde sign here. Any pin that has a tilde symbol on it is p capable, another document or another another table that is very useful to keep handy. Is this one here? It comes out of the datasheet and it's a summary of the various functionalities that are exposed at each pin. Awesome. Let's move on and have a look at the ESP 32 communications capabilities in the next project.

COMMUNICATIONS

Hi. This is a quick look at the various communications capabilities of the ESP 32 and that has to do with communications between things such as sensors and integrated circuits or other devices such as mobile phones and the Internet. In summary, these are the various communications options that come with the ESP 32. On the left, you have the main wireless capabilities, namely Wi-Fi and Bluetooth. And on the right you've got the wired capabilities which allow the ESP 32 to be connected to either other ISP through reducing microcontrollers or smaller devices like sensors. You've got three ESP channels. We've got two ice quit C channels, inter integrated circuit and two ice Kwid s, which is a lesser known communication technology. ICE quit s stands for

Inter i c for sound and it's an electrical cereal box just like the ice switch. C but typically used for connecting digital audio devices together. We also have three serial interfaces: an Ethernet Mac interface, a card bus controller area network bus, which is typically used in vehicle applications, automotive applications, and allow microcontrollers and devices to communicate with each other in cars.

ESP32 Communications

ESP32 offers multiple communications options

Wireless	Wired
Wifi	3 x SPI (Serial Peripheral Interface)
Bluetooth	2 x I^2C
	2 x I^2S
	3 x UART
	Ethernet MAC interface
	CAN 2.0
	IR (TX/RX)

And finally, we've got red to receive and transmit. And you can see how these capabilities are laid out in this functional block diagram. This is a close look at each one of these capabilities. Wi-Fi is integrated into the module and you find everything that you need to basically use and connect to a Wi-Fi network or to create a Wi-Fi hotspot. So you've got the antenna, the amplifier, various filters, power management and everything else that is needed as far as Wi-Fi protocols are concerned. We've got 802. 11 b, g n and 802. 11 and with up to 150 megabits per second bandwidth with support for Wi-Fi multimedia. You can find more details in the datasheet in Section 3.5. As far as the Bluetooth capability is concerned, the ESP 32is compliant with classic Bluetooth 4.2 and really Bluetooth low energy specifications. It costs one, two and three transmitters and it can simultaneously advertise and scan. Again, more details in that data sheet. And we've got three HP channels up to 80 megahertz in frequency. We've got three SPI channels XP, SPI and VSP, all of them up to 80 megahertz in frequency. The ESP32 contains two full I squared C bus interfaces and it can be configured to operate a SA master or a space standard or fast mode. We'll be using ICE quick C in this project to connect the ESP 32 to things such as sensors, in particular the PME 280 and the LCD screen with the ice Quick C backpack.

ESP32 Communications

I²C: Inter-integrated Circuit
Two I²C bus interfaces
Master or slave
Standard (100 Kbits/s) or Fast (400 Kbits/s)
Up to 5 MHz
7-bit or 10-bit addressing
Dual addressing

There's also two ice squid s interfaces which are typically used in audio applications and of course the ubiquitous UART universal and synchronous to receive the transmitter. Three of those interfaces are present. We can use them with any serial device in addition to the above. There's also the infrared receiver and transmit communication capability and an Ethernet Mac adapter so we can connect to a local network. As you can see, the ESP 32is quite a lot of capabilities to communicate with devices outside of 32, near or far away via the Internet. And we'll be demonstrating most of these capabilities in this project for the last project in this section, which is the next one. We'll have a look at the power options of your ISP. 32 queued.

POWER

Hi. This is the last project in this introductory section on the ESP 32, and we'll have a look at the three powering options. The first and most typical option is to use the USB ports, a micro USB port, which we use both for power and for serial communications and for uploading a sketch to the ISP. 32. Just plug that into your computer to use the P port or to a USB compatible power supply and you could go. The second option is to connect an external unregulated power supply to the five four valves pin and ground pins. Anything between around five and 212 volts should work, but it is best to keep it around 6 to 7 volts to avoid losing too much power Heat on the voltage regulator.

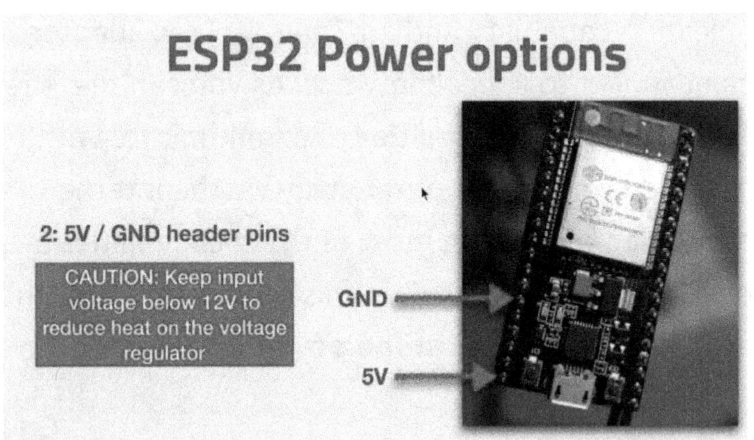
ESP32 Power options
2: 5V / GND header pins
CAUTION: Keep input voltage below 12V to reduce heat on the voltage regulator
GND
5V

So we've got an example here where I powered my ESP three to death kit using my bench power supply with a variety of input voltages. So you can see here I'm pairing it in at the moment at five fold, increasing the input voltage to six volts or so, and the seven volts eight, nine and ten volts and not going any further above it.

Another option that you have is to power your ESP three two using a 3.3 volt regulated power supply by connecting it to the 3.3 volt and ground pinch. The 3.3 volt pain is up top left of the board right next to the antenna. It can be very careful when you do that though because if you power yours especially this way, you're bypassing the onboard voltage regulator that is on board the death kit and therefore your module has no protection against overvoltage. It should be very careful to make sure that your input voltage is regulated and is safe.

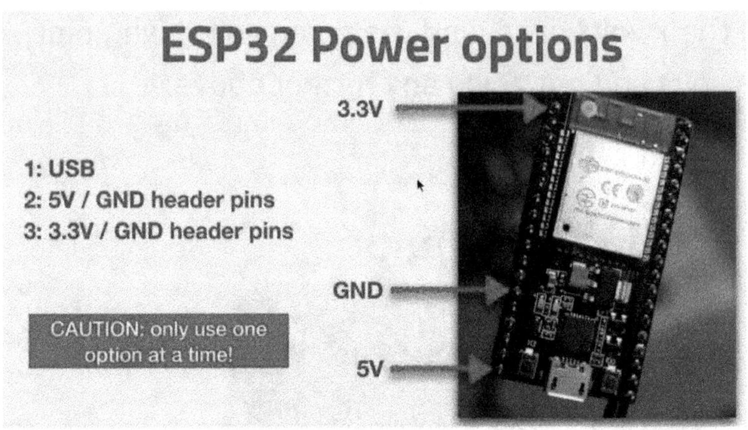

So these are the three power options. First via the USB port, second via unregulated voltage between five and 12 volts that goes through the ESP three to the delicate power regulator and three via the 3.3 volt pin. I can be very careful with that not to exceed the 3.3 volts limit or your HP three two modules will be damaged. Also be very, very careful to only use one of those options at the same time. So it did not power your USP three to save via the five caused pain using a ten volt input while at the same time you have the module connected to your computer via USB. That is a recipe for significant damage, at least to your module, if not also to your computer. Okay, so that's about it. With the introduction to the HP three two and the HP three two Dev Kit hardware, let's move on to the next section now we will start our hands-on experiments with the GPIO.

SETTING UP ESP32 IN THE ARDUINO IDE ON MAC OS

One of the really nice things about SB 52 is that it works with the Latino I.D. Not only that, but because of the support that the manufacturer has implemented for the Latino platform, we can use a lot of the existing card to, you know, libraries and infrastructure and hardware. That means that we can reuse what we already know in our work with their DNA. And they are doing it in particular with the SPF 32 and use all of the additional hardware capabilities that they expected to bring along. And the first thing that we need to do in order to be able to do such work is to install the SPF 50 to support the original I.D. And that's what we do in this project. I'll show you how to provide security support for the Latino I.D. first on the Mac and then in the next project in winters. In both cases, I assume that you really have the I.D. installed and working on your computer. And if you don't, then you can go to Arduino dot CC and the software downloads. You'll see this page and just download the installer file and install it. Once you have this done and you've got your Arduino I.D. Running in action is to go to GitHub and on GitHub at this location here, it's pretty easy for a speaker to use the repository that holds all the support files. It makes it possible to use the SPF 32, and I don't know if we need to copy these files into our. I do know how to fold them. This is a few ways by which you can do that, but by far the easiest is to do it via the port manager. And this feature works across platforms.

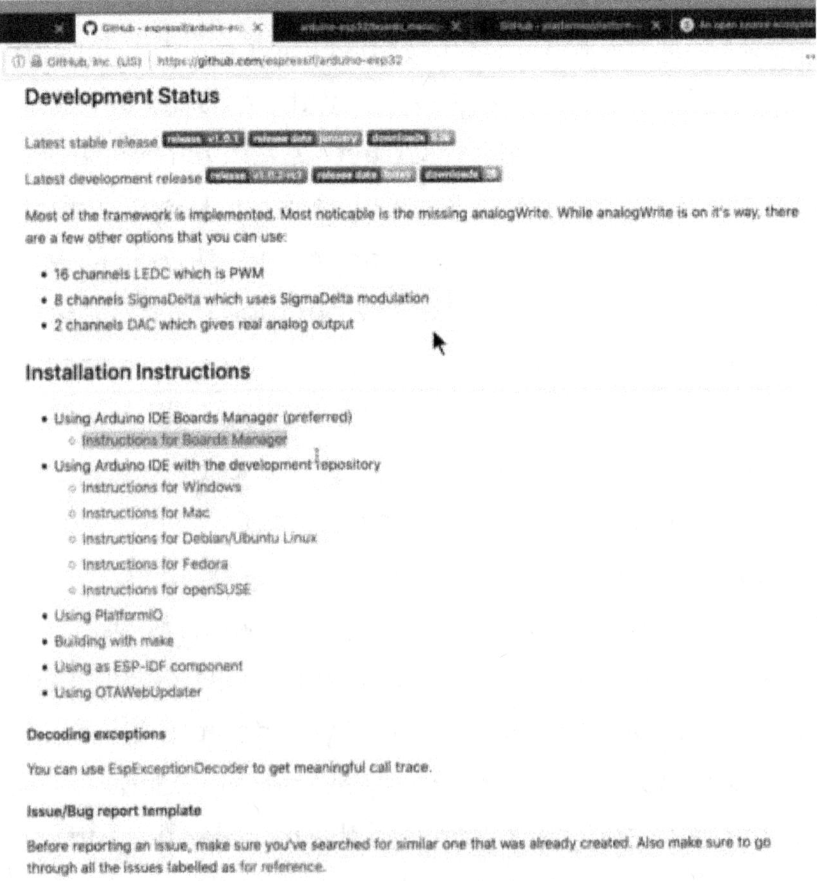
Development Status
Latest stable release
Latest development release
Most of the framework is implemented. Most noticable is the missing analogWrite. While analogWrite is on it's way, there are a few other options that you can use:
16 channels LEDC which is PWM
8 channels SigmaDelta which uses SigmaDelta modulation
2 channels DAC which gives real analog output
Installation Instructions
Using Arduino IDE Boards Manager (preferred)
Instructions for Boards Manager
Using Arduino IDE with the development repository
Instructions for Windows
Instructions for Mac
Instructions for Debian/Ubuntu Linux
Instructions for Fedora
Instructions for openSUSE
Using PlatformIO
Building with make
Using as ESP-IDF component
Using OTAWebUpdater
Decoding exceptions
You can use EspExceptionDecoder to get meaningful call trace.
Issue/Bug report template
Before reporting an issue, make sure you've searched for similar one that was already created. Also make sure to go through all the issues labelled as for reference.

So it's the same thing that you do when you're using the Mac or Windows or Linux, and that's how I'm going to do it as well in this project. So click on the instructions for which Manager Link will take you to this page here, which contains the instructions that we need. The first thing to do is to copy this hero, which points to a Jason file with instructions for the board manager to know which files to get, where to get it from, and where to store them locally. So I'm going to copy this here. You then go and Arduino preferences and paste that right here. So I already have it done. So click okay. And with that we can go and the Tools board and Boards manager and because of the hero that's pointing to the Jason file that I just added in the preferences can now go in search for is p32 that will bring up the only option available double check that up with the latest repository and click on install. So this is about 120 megabytes of data that I bought, which the manager will need to download and install. So can you give it a bit of time? And fast forward this part of the project and come back once the installation is complete. All right. So the support for the HP Veritas installed, let's check it out. So let's click on the tools menu and on the board can see that we now have support for a load of HP three two boards. The very large variety they want to be using in this project is the stock standard, ESP three to dev module so I can select it here and that will bring up all the configuration for this particular board and you can see it listed here as well.

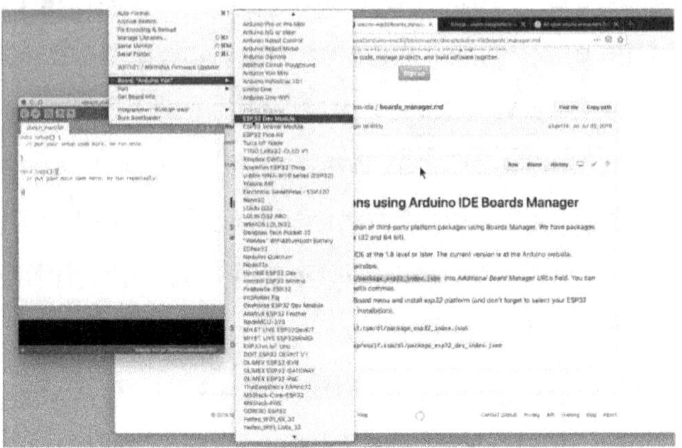

So all of these options are correct. We don't have to change anything here. Those correspond exactly to the stock standard SB 32 dev module that'll be using another thing that we can look at. Is this going to be an example? And then down here at the bottom of the examples window or dropdown I should say are a load of examples for the HP 32 and many of those will be playing with in the later sections as we are starting to explore and discover the capabilities of the DSP. 32. Another thing is back on the tools, the ports menu. Right now I don't have my HP 30 connected, so it's not showing up. But beginning with the next section you'll be able to see your HP three two listed here just like it happens with any other normal doing or regular high doing, you should say. And the last thing is, I want to show you where the packages or the where the data that provide the HP three to support the files that make up the support are stored. So in my case, I want to gain proficiency. You see here there's a path I specified and then you use a folder library of 15 and that at this location, which we are right here in the finder, you see packages below packages, you can see all the files that make up the issue security support. So that's what it all goes. If you're wondering, one thing before we go to the next project is to just make a brief mention of the alternative integrated development environment that you can use with the ISP 32, which is actually one of many, but one very popular such platform outside of the know it is platform IO IDE, so very, very popular among programmers of any kind and not specifically are doing a program. This is a general purpose integrated development environment with some really awesome features and it's worth looking at. I'm going to be using platform IO IDE for the SB 32 in the next course that I'm designing at the moment. It's going to be a follow up course to the present course, which is for beginners, for people new to the SB 32. So for the intermediate level, SB 42 makers will be using platform IO ID instead of the original idea, and that will unlock a few not necessarily complicated but definitely powerful features that can make use of OC. And with this said, if you want to know how to install SB three D support on Windows, check out the next project. Otherwise you can skip it and move on to the next section where we'll start doing some experimentation with his P3 two and beginning to explore the GPIO capabilities.

SETTING UP ESP32 IN THE ARDUINO IDE ON WINDOWS 10

All right. In this project, I'm going to show you how to set up the sp3 to support the dino I.D. on windows in particular. I'm using Windows ten for this demonstration. As I said in a previous project, the HP three two is an advanced hardware platform for Internet of Things applications. And one of its great advantages compared to competitors is that it's perfectly compatible with their platform. And this means that you can use your existing DINO knowledge with the HP three to even take advantage of the HP 32 additional hardware capabilities. So the first step towards making it possible to develop applications for the HP three two in the DINO, is to install the ESP three to support the DINO idea. And this one could do right away. Before we begin, I assume that you already have the dino ID installed in your computer and if you don't have it, just go to w w don't. In a dodge cc, click on software download and download the appropriate version of the ID in your I.D. for your operating system. All right. Let's continue with this. So the files that you need to install in order to add his P3 to support for your identity are here on GitHub. And this is the location where you can find them.

There's a few different ways by which you can install them on your computer, but the easiest one is to use the I do know I.D. Ports Manager feature. And in the past, especially for the HP 8266, this was a little bit more involved. We had to do a little bit more manual copying and configuration. But things have improved a lot since then. So I'm going to open up this link in a new tab. Here it is and follow these simple instructions. So the windows side by side and start my I.D.. All right. And the first thing I should do is to copy this serial, which points to a Jason file that contains hardware configuration information and go into files, preferences and paste these your real down here and additional ports click on. Okay. And then the next thing to do is to go to the tools, go to the board's manager and search for s p 32. Okay, Wait for a few seconds for the index to update. Okay. And he p three, two, one. Make sure that I've got the latest version selected and click on install it. You saw that there's a 31 megabyte file to download all the files and get a bit of time to complete that and fast forward this bit and come back once the download installation is complete. Okay, so that is done close. The manager will look at what we've got now. First let's go to the tools menu and under boards we'll see that we've got or we should have it.

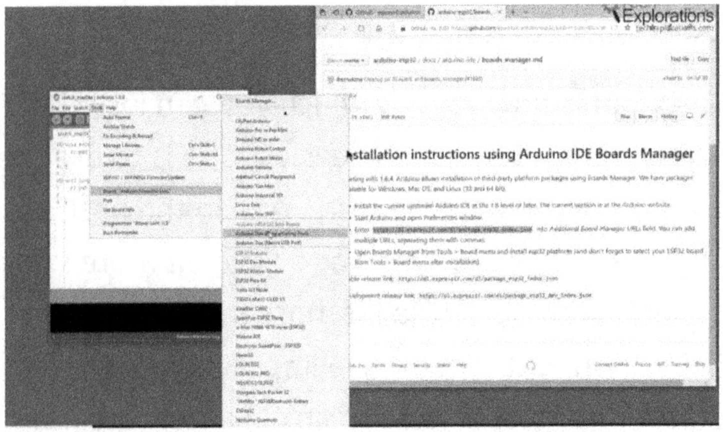

There we go. We've got a whole new section that contains various ISP three ports. Hey care. So the one that will be using this project is the stock standard SPC dev module. When you click onto this and you see that now we've got a few new options for the hardware that we've selected, upload, speed, frequency, etc. all these default to the correct values for the SPC dev module that we've selected here. If you have selected one of the others, then these will also update appropriately. So we are not going to have to make any changes to any of those settings. I don't have an especially two modules connected, so it doesn't appear in this in the port dropdown, but we'll do that in the next section when we start with a few demonstrations. Another thing to look at is if you go to the file menu and the examples, you try it again, you'll see that we've got a lot of very specific few examples here and we'll be playing with those in later sections starting from the very next section where we'll have an example of how to use HPR. All right, So that's about it. Let's move on to the next section. Now we'll start playing around with some of the examples and becoming familiar with the new hardware.

INSTALL THE DRIVERS CP21012 USB CHIP

Before we start experimenting with the ISP three to Dev Kit. Wanted to mention one issue that a lot of people come across and that has to do with the sheer number of different development kits for the XP 32 and the small differences between them. One of those differences has to do with the chip that is used to implement the USP two UART Bridge, which enables the USB programmability of the board. So this chip here on my board, which is just a stock standard, this is said before, it requires a driver that typically is not installed by default on Windows or Mac OS computers and therefore has to be installed manually and without installing, this particular driver will not be able to upload a sketch to the board.

So my particular board uses the c P 20 10xa driver or in particular the cp2102 driver in your case, probably something like that. This is a popular low cost. You want to use the P bridge and chip and if you want to dig in a little bit more in this area, then you can go to sp3 to net. So this is the year where we can go and you can have a look at what the variations of the various uses are to you, what chip bridges are available and you can find information in here about which driver is appropriate for your operating system. In my case, I plugged in my development kit, VSP, to my computer. Then I went to my ED. I'd had a look at tools and board and I couldn't find the port to which my kid is connected. So that was a little bit of work in the documentation of this board. I discovered that I need to install the CP 21 through two drivers for Mac OS. So this is a place where you can do that.

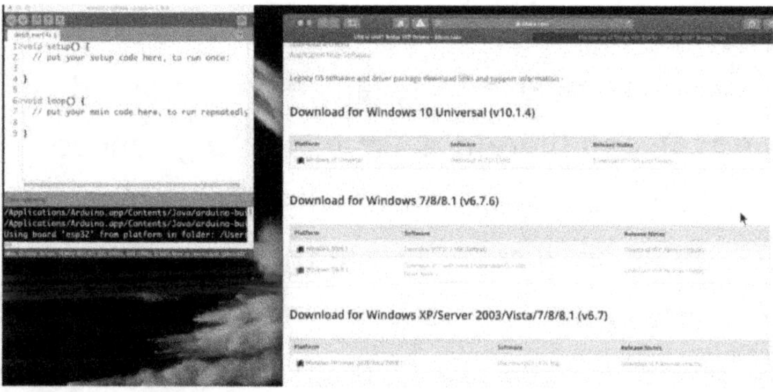

This driver comes for a variety of operating systems. Go here, download the one for your operating system and install it and restart your. I do not. So I'm going to do that right now because of how many different drivers are out there and the differences between the operating systems and the exact installation procedure. I'm not going to record this bit. I'm going to install it and come back in a few minutes to see how the port to which the kit is connected can now be accessed. Do it. Okay, so I installed this driver on my computer. It required a restart of my operating system as well. And now I can go back to my I.D., click on the Tools menu, have a look inside the port, and you can see that there is the port to which my kit is connected. So let's try an upload. Going to click on the upload button. I need to save this sketch first. Okay. There's nothing in this sketch. Just totally empty out doing your sketch. Just want to verify that I can actually upload to the dashboard. All right. So you can see that it is uploading and 100% completed and reset itself so the sketch will start running. Okay, So this is a little test that verifies to me that my death kit can be programmed by my Arduino I.D. and therefore, I'm happy to go ahead now in the next section and start doing a few experiments before you move on. Just verify that this also works for you. I've got my Windows virtual environment here and if I'm going to try the same thing, I'm going to connect the use be bridge of my death kit to Windows and make sure that I can see it. So see, I can't see it. So I'm going to have to follow this same process here for Windows ten in order to be able to program my XP three to Dev Kid under Winters. I'm going to do that as well and come back to verify that before I continue with the next section.

DIGITAL OUTPUT LED

In this project, we'll start the practical exploration of the features of the SB 32 dev kit and the first experiment or example that we look at is a traditional blinking entity that we are familiar with from How do we know? We're going to use pretty much the knowledge that we have from the author, you know, and without much more will be able to use the USP 32 to drive this entity. This is going to give us the opportunity to also learn a few things about how the chip heroes work on the ESP 32 and how they correspond to the things that we know about GPIO from the ADRENO. So let's have a look at this little example and then as we go ahead, we'll have the opportunity to talk more about the details. So what I've got in this little example is a single entity connected to a 230 ohm resistor. You can use any value between, say, 230 to 500 ohms, and this is still going to work in the entity. It's going to be bright. Don't go lower than that, because then you'll be drawing too much current from the ESP 32. So I've connected the anode of the LCD to one of the GPIO on the expected two and the cathode to the Blu-ray. Or would you stick around the trail which then connects to one of the available ground pins on the ESP 32.

The schematic looks like this. Very simple, so I've chosen GPIO 32. I could have taken any of the others, but with some exceptions that I'm going to talk about in a minute. And that goes through to the anode and via the resistor to one of the crown pins. And you've got the one ground pin here, and there's another one here and here now. So let's talk about pins. Throughout this project. I'll be using this pin map that I've put together. And in this PIN map, I've noted down the most important functionalities of each pin and remember that each pin, as we said in the past, in the previous project, has got multiple capabilities and not all of them are marked here to put this map together. I've taken information from the data sheet of the ESP 32 so you can look at the details in this data sheet, but these are the functionalities that we'll be working with in this project and the ones that are found most useful but most commonly used. So it's good to have a quick reference in this format to note up here that a bunch of pins in GPI use which are at the end of the board and on the top left side are only able to be used as inputs. So GPI was 34353936 and can only be used as inputs. Therefore I wouldn't be able to use any of them to drive my ability.

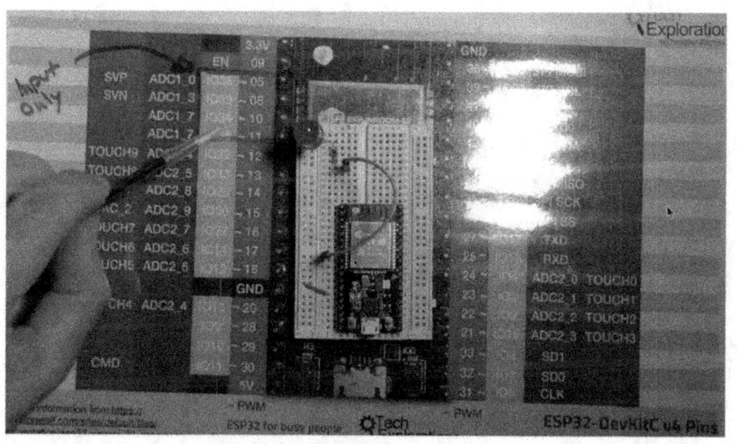

But this can be used for other things. It can be used as outputs, for example, to see these little tilde marks gyros that can be used for a p.w aim, which is something that we're going to do in the next project and many other functions, but not for an output. So this input on B, So I've chosen PIN three, which is one, two, three, 45678, eight.

So I'm counting the pins on this side. Which brings me to another little piece of advice, if I can call it that, that I can give. You have connected the ESP three to the death kit on my breadboard like this and pushed it to the side so that I get two exposed pins on each column on this side. Since this is the side that I actually want to use for the next few experiments, I'm not going to be able to plug anything on this side because there's nothing available and everything is just down inaccessible at the moment. I've also pushed the use based side of the ESP 32 up towards the edge of the breadboard so that the first pin aligned too with the marking number 1341 to plug something in to pin say eight. I can quickly do that and just plug it in. Say one, two, three, four, count from the bottom that is from this side here. I'll be able to just count on my map and then quickly plug in the jumper wire to the appropriate pin. So let's try that again. So I want to plug something into PIN 33 so that it's one, two, three, four, five, six, seven, eight, nine, ten, 11, 12. Number 12 from the bottom. So that is number 12 where I have plugged in the downward of the LP. Then via the blue rail, I connect the cover to ground, which is this pin right here. One, two, three, four, five, six. So that is right on two six. Okay, so let's have a look at the sketch. Now just go over to my computer and instead of loading a pre-wedding sketch, we are going to load one in the blink example and then modify it slightly to get it to work with. It is fitted to circle two examples. Get the basics link and this is the classic. And in a blink example, the board that I have does have a couple of these, but none of them are connected to any of the HPR. There should be some indicator early days for power and for activity for the serial port. So this build in constant doesn't translate to an actual building head on the board. So I'm going to have to replace that. And that's the only modification I'm going to do in this example. So let's declare a new constant. We only need an eight bit byte here.

```
  by Scott Fitzgerald
  modified 2 Sep 2016
  by Arturo Guadalupi
  modified 8 Sep 2016
  by Colby Newman

  This example code is in the public domain.

  http://www.arduino.cc/en/Tutorial/Blink
*/

const byte

// the setup function runs once when you press reset or power the board
void setup() {
  // initialize digital pin LED_BUILTIN as an output.
  pinMode(LED_BUILTIN, OUTPUT);
}

// the loop function runs over and over again forever
void loop() {
  digitalWrite(LED_BUILTIN, HIGH);   // turn the LED on (HIGH is the voltage level)
  delay(1000);                       // wait for a second
  digitalWrite(LED_BUILTIN, LOW);    // turn the LED off by making the voltage LOW
```

So ready to go for an integer and let's call this AM any day. It's a cheap chip any day. Hi ho. And here, let's go back to the map and have a look at where I have connected my any day. So I've oriented my breadboard with his B on it so that it corresponds nicely with the image that I've got here on my map. And the antenna's up here, the antenna is up here and now I can compare the names of the pins to find out the GPIO number that I need to put into my sketch. So I'm looking at number 12 from the bottom. As I said earlier, this is GPA or IO. I made it a little shorter here. Said a bit of space 33. So just start typing a 33 in here and then copy the new constant for the pin across to place a previous variable. And that is about it. That's all you need to do. Essentially just find the right GPO port, place that into the appropriate variable constant in this case in the sketch and you're good to go. I'm going to plug it into his computer too. Now I've uploaded this sketch earlier so you can see that it's already working. Let's do this whole thing from the beginning. So in tools, make sure that you have selected the appropriate dev kit. For me, it's the ECP three to generic dev module. This board doesn't even have a brand totally generic, so make sure this is selected. Then everything else, once you select the board, everything else should automatically go to the defaults, which are correct. And then go for the serial port. Select that and then click on upload. My board does not reset automatically. When I do an upload, I can go in to load the bootloader and start receiving the sketch. So I need to press the boot button and hold it down until I can see the writing has started. And with that completed I can see that the ADT is blinking. So that was easy, wasn't it? Now let's take this one step further. Your next project did mention that any pin with a little tilde mark is capable of p w m so let's try that in the next project. Let's make this any day to defeat.

PWM AND LED

Hi. In the previous project, you've learned how to get the LTE connected to speed through to blink. And in this project, I'll show you how to make it fade out by using the p w m capability after each p32. The addition, of course, can also output p w m but as you'll see in this project, the PSP three two has got several additional capabilities in its hardware that the actor actually shared with the maker at Mega three $0.28 cannot even imagine. Hence, you will see very, very soon. So first of all, let's have a quick look at the hardware which is very simple. As you can see, the same hardware and configuration that we used in the previous project with the blinking LTE. And then we'll move straight to the software and see what those additional capabilities in software look like. So I've got the LTE connected to PIN Chip I over 13. Let's check out the schematic. Sorry, 33 I should say so. 32 and double check that I've got it connected to 33 which is OC some little correction on my diagram in my software. I've got the LTE connected to 33, not 32, but either one is OC as you can see from the map. Shouldn't matter a bit. I have both pinch 33 and 30 2 p.m.. Capable so you can choose one for the other and that's about it. I have got the cathode of the entity connected to one of the electricity to ground, hence.

Okay, you plug it in and there's the LTE fading notion and look at the sketch that makes it possible. I want to compare the sketch that you're looking at right now, which is the p 32 version of the fading LCD sketch with that of the administering the adreno good. Two examples basics in Fade. We'll see the example sketch and here you see the analog write function. We pass it to the ping that we want, which we have the LCD connected to, and then the p definitely m values the brightness, which is a value between 0 to 255 and then we can change the value stored in the brightness variable using some kind of loop. In this case, we just throw a little addition here inside the loop so we can on the flight change the brightness of this little axis. And we're up here with the pin configured. This output, the DSP 32 doesn't have access to the same Arduino function. The analog right. It's a library that provides a new different function called altitude. Not that one. This one here is called entity C, Right. And to it we pass a channel number and then the value for the brightness. And this is where the power of the.

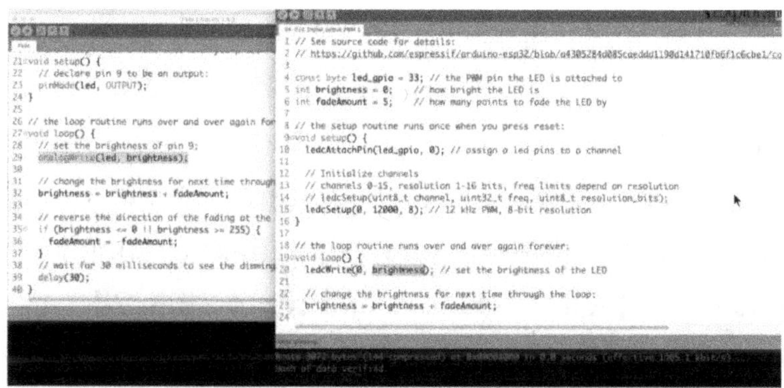

Speaker two When it comes to creating pwm signals comes in because the channel can be one of many, as we'll see in the documentation. It's one of 16 channels that can be attached to any pwm capable pin, and then the brightness can be any number configurable. Again, up to 16 bits that is the resolution. So let's have a look at the documentation to get some more details about what is happening here. So this is a documentation in that you can find a printed data sheet and search for P.W and you'll see examples that describe the paint at the end functionality to drive motors and to drive any DS. So let's have a look. And the diagram shows us that there is a dedicated hardware module inside the microcontroller for BW and this is where the 16 p.m. channels are implemented in this block right here. And then continue searching. Okay. So this is a description of the approach with the modulation capability. So we've got dedicated timers for P.W and each one generates a waveform for 1 p.m. channel. And more interesting is this section here. So the P.W controller, the block that you saw, the block diagram set up can generate 16 independent channels which you can attach to any P.W and compatible PIN. There is a 90 megahertz clock. Driving those channels is a 20 bit timer, and the duty cycle can be up to 16 bits within one millisecond period. So something similar happens with a notice note, a section somewhere close, but it's about the same. And you can see here I got back a bit. Any GPIO pin can be used to drive any ds and attach each one of the 16 P.W and generators. And the same thing happens with the motor.

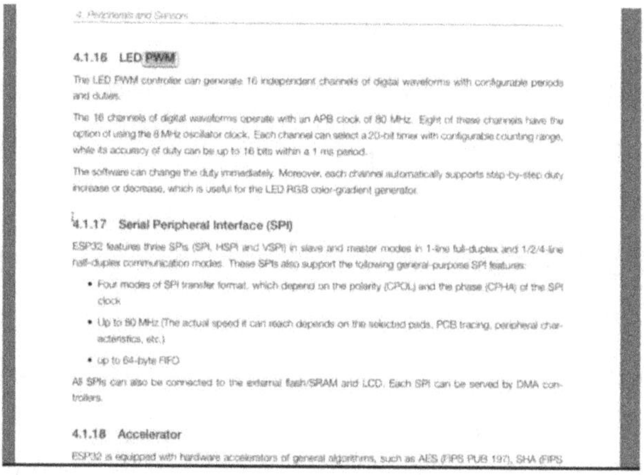

4. Peripherals and Sensors

4.1.16 LED PWM

The LED PWM controller can generate 16 independent channels of digital waveforms with configurable periods and duties.

The 16 channels of digital waveforms operate with an APB clock of 80 MHz. Eight of these channels have the option of using the 8 MHz oscillator clock. Each channel can select a 20-bit timer with configurable counting range, while its accuracy of duty can be up to 16 bits within a 1 ms period.

The software can change the duty immediately. Moreover, each channel automatically supports step-by-step duty increase or decrease, which is useful for the LED RGB color-gradient generator.

4.1.17 Serial Peripheral Interface (SPI)

ESP32 features three SPIs (SPI, HSPI and VSPI) in slave and master modes in 1-line full-duplex and 1/2/4-line half-duplex communication modes. These SPIs also support the following general-purpose SPI features:

- Four modes of SPI transfer format, which depend on the polarity (CPOL) and the phase (CPHA) of the SPI clock
- Up to 80 MHz (The actual speed it can reach depends on the selected pads, PCB tracing, peripheral characteristics, etc.)
- up to 64-byte FIFO

All SPIs can also be connected to the external flash/SRAM and LCD. Each SPI can be served by DMA controllers.

4.1.18 Accelerator

ESP32 is equipped with hardware accelerators of general algorithms, such as AES (FIPS PUB 197), SHA (FIPS

Any GPIO pin can be used to draw motors. And I've got Alexa to show you how to do that with motors. Okay, now let's have a look at the sketch, then repeat in more detail and walk through it. The source code that shows you how to use the function such as DC right and DC set up and any DC attached. You can find it here. So this is the GitHub repository for specific and specifically for the Arduino. And you speak of 32 support for source code. And here in this header file and this is the ESD three two how Ellie DC talks head to head of file you can see the available public functions. So we've got a setup function that accepts a channel. The frequency that we want within the range that is possible and the resolution. So that's what I do right here. I call this function and set up the Channel zero at 12 kilohertz of 12,000 hertz and I give it an eight bit resolution. So the number that I provide for the brightness has to be between two zero and 255. I also need to attach a channel to a physical pin. So I do that using the LP attachment, hence making that a bit bigger. So do that in the ADT attach pin function. You. So this function accepts a GPIO and a channel and that's what I do in the set of functions. At the beginning of the setup function I call Ellie d attach pin, I pass the GPIO that I want to get connected to, which is 33 and the channel. And this could have been either a zero or a one or two. Now up to 15, because I've got 15 channels available for this. That information is also here as well as in the datasheet.

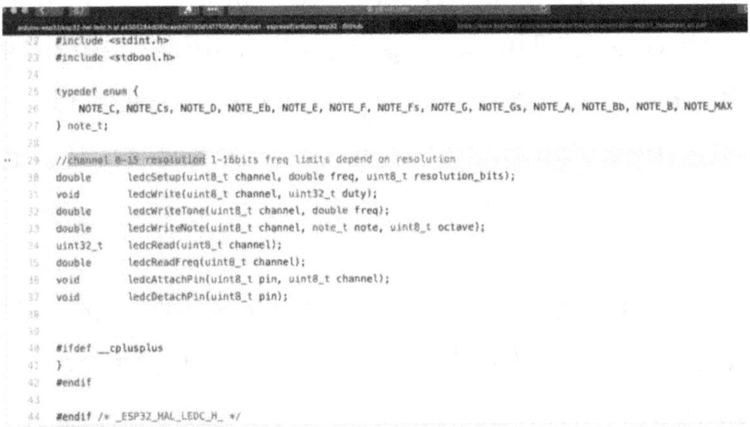

```
#include <stdint.h>
#include <stdbool.h>

typedef enum {
    NOTE_C, NOTE_Cs, NOTE_D, NOTE_Eb, NOTE_E, NOTE_F, NOTE_Fs, NOTE_G, NOTE_Gs, NOTE_A, NOTE_Bb, NOTE_B, NOTE_MAX
} note_t;

//channel 0-15 resolution 1-16bits freq limits depend on resolution
double      ledcSetup(uint8_t channel, double freq, uint8_t resolution_bits);
void        ledcWrite(uint8_t channel, uint32_t duty);
double      ledcWriteTone(uint8_t channel, double freq);
double      ledcWriteNote(uint8_t channel, note_t note, uint8_t octave);
uint32_t    ledcRead(uint8_t channel);
double      ledcReadFreq(uint8_t channel);
void        ledcAttachPin(uint8_t pin, uint8_t channel);
void        ledcDetachPin(uint8_t pin);


#ifdef __cplusplus
}
#endif

#endif /* _ESP32_HAL_LEDC_H_ */
```

So I've got the channel attached to the IO that I want to use. So at this point my p m function as implemented with the ADT is ready to go. So let's get into the loop, the loop instead of analog. Right. We'll use Ellie DC right. The function here is this: in the header file it accepts the channel number and the duty cycle. So the channel number is whatever I set up here in Ellie DC set up and then the brightness, which is the duty cycle, has to be within the range of the eight bits that I selected and configured this particular channel to use. So it's going to be a number between zero and 255 and that's it right here. And the rest of the content in the loop function is exactly the same as in the traditional duty. No fading Ellie example. So the result that you see here is four and I think I was playing around with a four kilo heads frequency on this call for 12 kilohertz and upload the sketch, double check. I've got the right port. Yep. Good. So upload a sketch and see what it looks like. Save it and you can hold down the boot button to get the sketch to upload. Okay. All right. So this is a 12 kilohertz P.W signal at eight bits. Another thing that I can do is I can use my oscilloscope to see the end value and visualize that I can compare it with the signal visualized signal of another frequency. Let's make it six kilohertz. So let's check it out. Okay, Turn on my oscilloscope and reposition camera. Sure. Let's connect the probes. I'm going to use a jump wire to take a signal p.w signal into the blue channel and then the ground. I'm just going to press on the auto button and get the oscilloscope to find the signal and display it. And there it is, which reduces the horizontal scale so we can see it increasingly decreasing. So this is what a pwm signal looks like on the SBC two and 12 kilohertz and eight bits. So just a little modification. Let's say that we'd like this signal to have a smaller frequency, but the same size of the duty cycle, still eight bit resolution. What will that look like and what will the D fade on and also look like as well? Something that pressing the boot pattern. Okay, I can see looks wider now. Still the same resolution, sort of same step increase in the duty cycle. So you can experiment with that. You can try out different frequencies, different resolutions, see what the effect that has on the LCD. And we're going to experiment with this a bit later when we start, when we do some experimentation with notice. Also, let's move on to the next project now where we're playing around with an IGP any day.

RGB LED WITH PWM

In this project, I'll show you how to use your ESP three to digitize a RTP artificiality, which is really just taking what you learned in the previous project two steps further. The first step, of course, is to use what you learned to drive the three components, three click components of energy purity using three of the Espace digital paints. And the other thing that I'm going to show you is how the additional pins are mapped into the spins in one of the heads of files in the ESP two and we now support source code. So to begin with, take a look at what the outcome of this little experiment is going to be like. And I've got it here powered up. You can see I've got a common node,

IGP entity connected, producing a variety of colors. It's actually cycling, cycling through all of the colors of the spectrum. And in my case, I'm using a common node elite.

So the lone pin for this elite is the common anode. You need to then figure out what the other pins are, which is very easy with a button battery. But if you have a common cathode LCD, again, you can do this experiment. Just you need to make a few little adjustments on these shows, on the wiring that I'm going to show you in a minute. So let's begin with the wiring and explain how it's all connected and what to do if you have a common cathode. IGP, LCD So here is my current anode and I'm going to use a button battery to figure out the pins that control the different composite colors of the IGP. So I'm going to orient my battery so that the positive is on the inside. And since I know that this is a common anode, I'm going to touch the plus side. So here's a plus side to the longer lead pane of the chargeability. So this brings into contact the negative side of the battery with the right most penultimate and I'm getting a red color here so we write this down in a little diagram. So this is the red, this is the common honor. And then I've got another two. I'm going to figure out right away what they are. So can I take my battery, flip it around so that the positive is always towards the anode and tested. So this is the green. So making sure that the two pins on the other side of the left side do not come into contact. So pull one away. Just keep one pin connected and anode to yes the tricky, but you can do it without bending the pinch too much, tricking. So these two together give me green. Right.

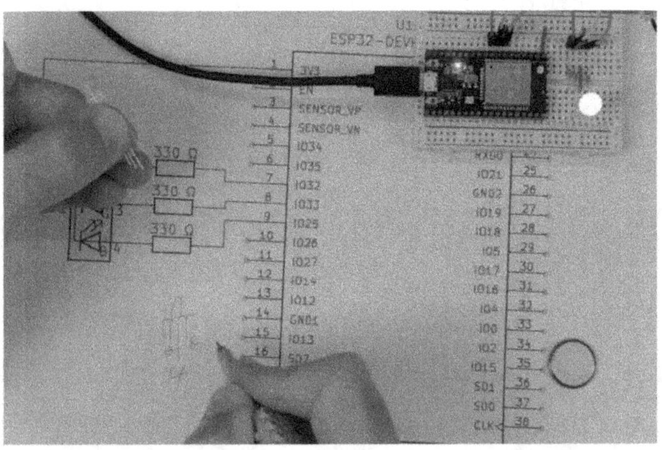

So this is the green and the last one. Right. Green is blue. So this gives me information. I need to go ahead and make my connections in the schematic, in my wiring. Okay. So I'm using a 330 ohm current limiting resistor for each of the components. I connect the red to pin three to green to point three, three and blue to pin 25 so that they are adjacent. And that's what I've done here. Let's bring up my pin map oriented appropriately so I have pins 32, 33 and 25 that drive the three components, the common anode, which is this pin right here. I've connected that via a couple of jumpers to the red power rail, and that goes to the 3.3 volts. So if you have a common cathode, then what you do is instead of connecting the a common pin, which in that case is going to be the common cathode to the red power rail and then to the 3.3 volts, you connect it to the blue power rail and then to the ground the pin. And there's one little modification that you need to do in the sketch that I'm going to show you right away. So that's all there is to do. In regards to the hardware. It's pretty simple. Let's move on to the firmware now. So the sketch that I'm going to show you is a slightly modified version of the sample sketch that you can access via file example and go to SB 32 and it's somewhere here you go. This one here is actually any. DC Right. IGP So I've just taken that sketch and added some documentation. As you can see. Here's the sketch that we used in the previous project with a single red any day. It's exactly the same thing that we are doing here with the IGP. It's just everything is done in threes. So we have the three days and we define the pins to which each component is connected to. And I'm going to talk more about what the A4, A5 and 18 notation constants actually say in this project in just a minute. Then we define the channels, we'll use channels 1 to 3 use channels arbitrarily, anywhere from 0 to 15, so say zero and 14, and then assign those to the pins down here, attach them to the pins down here.

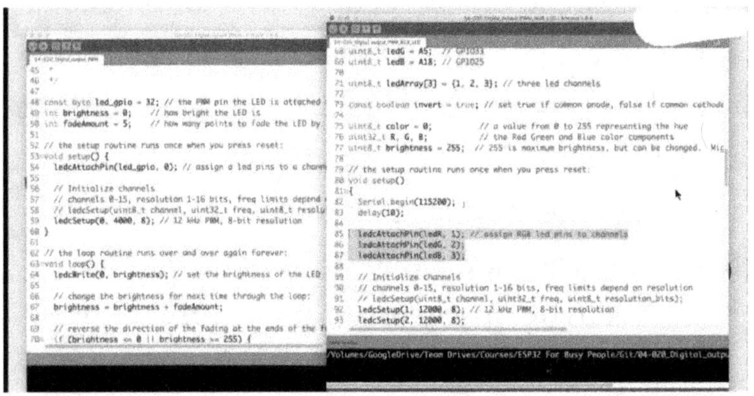

So we follow the exact same process. The only difference that is quite significant is that because we now want to create colors out of this LCD, not just bleed them on enough. We need some way of translating a color or color code to an g B value. So individual values for the red, green and blue for the P definitely M values for those individual colors. And to do that, we used this function here Hue to IGP. So we take a single value for the hue and then we are breaking that into the three components for the three basic composite lattice colors of the IGP entity. So you can take inside this function if you want, and understand exactly how it works. But the main idea here is it will use the hue, which is this representation of the color spectrum here. And each color has got a number that represents it. For example, zoom in. You see that red actually goes to this side of the red. Red is represented by the color code 360 and blue is represented by about 230 and so on. And then we can use an algorithm as just as we do in this function to convert the hue into and P.W and value for the red P.W and value for the blue and P.W and value for the green. And it's also provisioned here for your entity being common anode or common cathode. So see somewhere here because it will invert variable diffusion, common anode makes the true otherwise makes it false. And what that is going to do in the hue two IGP function is going to invert the colors that come out so that you have the correct color regardless of whether you're using a common anode or common cathode. IGP entity. The last thing that I want to show you is which is actually very important, not just for this example, but for everything that requires GPIO in the HP 32 other mappings. So because we're using the adding of plot form and we want to reuse our Arduino knowledge with the HP three to the support source code that we installed in the ITP contains PIN mappings.

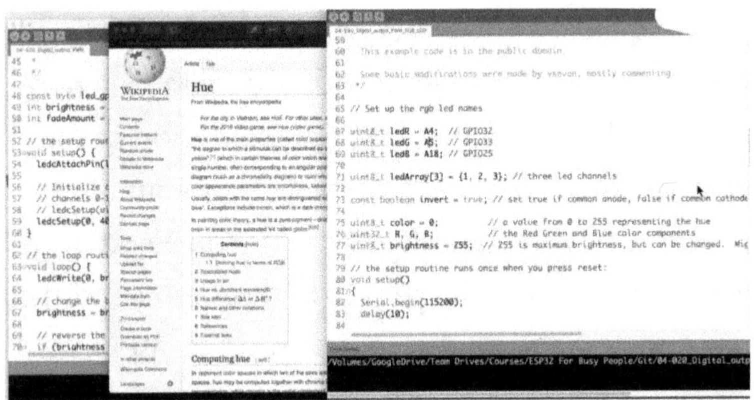

So mappings between the Arduino and the ESP 32. And that's why in this case we denoted the pin to which the red component of fear is connected to is a full and then for the green F five or 18 instead we could have just said like we did in the previous project, 32 like that. And this would be using the HP 32 pin maps, but just to show you how we can now use the PIN maps instead and make this a little bit more familiar. So these are defined in the I do know as story in the I do not speak for source code pins underscore Arduino don't page file and go to GitHub and have a look at this file. You'll see that I got all the pins listed here. So here is a zero which corresponds to pin three six, a 3.39 in the P world, A for each three, two and so on. We've got definitions and mappings I should say, for the transmit and receive pin c s t a for our squared see God and spy for the down which code the touch points. So quick look at the map you'll see. And I've got projects that describe how the touch pins work. But you can see here we've got patch zero in the map and that corresponds to GPIO and number four which is listed in this file. And finally, the digital to analog converters, which I have at projects that describe how to use those as well. So that's where you can find this original information. But at the end of the day, it's up to you whether you want to use the ordinal mappings or the BSP mappings. Before I upload the sketch, just to verify that it's two works or there haven't been any changes, I just want to also show you where the location of this file in your installation falls down on your computer? So since we installed it in the Mac OS system, if you go into libraries folder under your account name, then look for Arduino one five Inside that there's packages inside that there is the p32 in addition to the three no folder with support for the editor platform and hardware and you've got the ESP three to a folder inside it, you've got the hardware support in it, you've got the HP 321.01, which is the version of the source code that we're working variants. This is where you've got support for all the various HP 32 boards that are available, and I'm using the generic one. So that is P3 two. And in this pinch underscore, I do not do a page which contains the mapping set I showed you on GitHub. Okay. So that's about it. Let's upload make sure that everything is in order should this be connected to the correct you add and then upload. You hold down the boot button to get the HP three two into the upload mode. Great. Okay. So this gets started executing again. I can also use a serial monitor because this sketch has started. The serial port has spent 115,002 hundred boards and location and it will limit a few messages at the beginning of each loop and tell us what it does. Just give some information about its execution. So it's going through the first loop now. And on this 255 to 10 and morning tenant mortuary, then a zero could turn it off and then it goes through the color loop. This is great. I hope this was useful. So let's move on to the next project. Now we will talk about the analog pins and the capabilities.

DIGITAL INPUT WITH BUTTON

Hi. In this project, I'll show you how to read the state of a push button using your ISP. 32. In previous projects, you learned how to control the state of anything. And I'm going to use the LCD in this project to display visually the state of the button. Having a quick look at the map of the ISP 30 to the pin map just to quickly let you know that we can control an LCD using any of the digital output pins. So have quite a large selection of those pins chip behaves. It can use the same pins as inputs and use them therefore to read the state of push buttons. And in an upcoming project, I'm also going to show you how to read the state of Potentiometers. But in addition to those, just remember that we've got four pins up here.

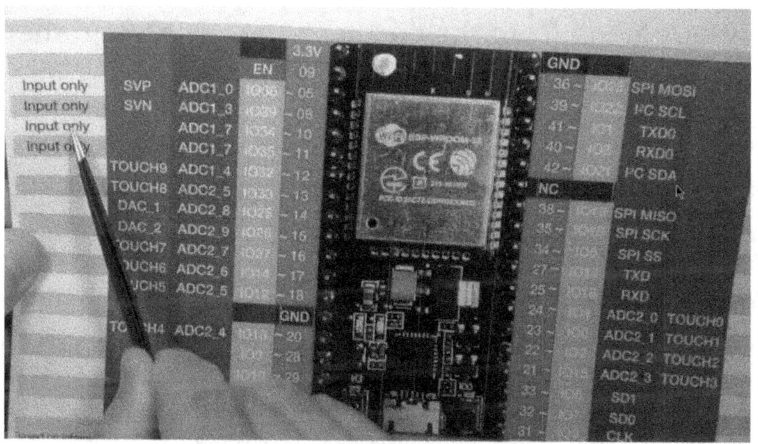

So these are pins, 36, 60, 35, which can only be used as inputs. In addition to some other capabilities that they have, such as the SVP industry. And this is something I'm going to show you in a later section. So in this project, the schematic, the wiring schematic that I have assembled here in my breadboard is that I've got a push button. The one of the pins of a push button is connected to the 3.3 fourths pin, which is pin number one to sort of place it like that. They can see them in parallel. So here's a push button. I've got its pin. Its side pins called this pin number two connected to 3.3 volts, 3.3 volt trail right here. And then the other pin is connected to pin number three. Yes.

You see the board in this direction, which is this pin right here, which is digital pin 36 and the pin diagram. And that's how I've referred to this pin in the in the program, in the sketch, I also have used a painkiller on pull down resistor because PIN number one is the one that I'm using to take the reading from the part into the HP 32, and then I'm pulling this pin down to the ground to crown the pin, which is this pin right here, Crown cradle, so that when the button is not pressed, it's just floating the is. We started to get a definite ground level reading here so that, as I said, the reading is not floating too. Don't forget this. Pull down the resistor. And then for the LCD, the situation is very simple. I've got a 330 on current limiting resistor and via it the leak is connected to pin GPIO, I should say appropriate theta in series with a resistor and then the cathode of the letter goes to ground.

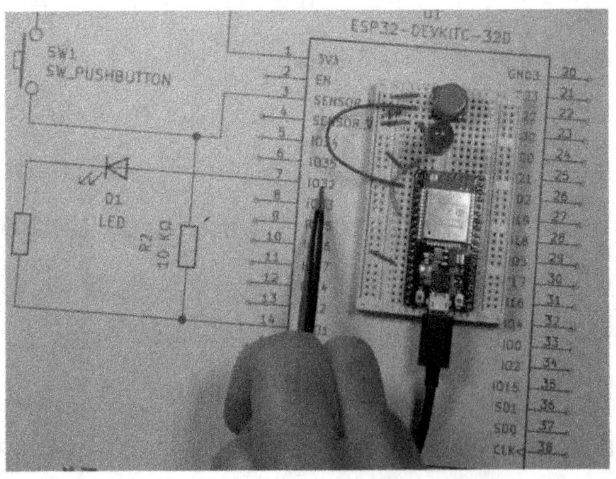

All right, so I've got this sketch running on my HP 32. I press the button litigation, let it go depressed, the LTE goes off. It's exactly the kind of wiring that you would do with the Arduino and having a look at the sketch. So here's a sketch for this example. You see that pretty much everything here is, as you would expect them to be in the sketch. There's really no difference. I've got two pins, one for the LTE, one for the button. I've got a variable to hold to the current state of the button. Then in the setup method, I initialize the two pins, one at an output for the LCD and one is an input and in the loop I'm constantly taking a reading using the digital read function for the button and depending on what that state is, what the current value of the button state variable is at the on or off. It's pretty simple, as you can see to take a reading from a button in this way. So let's move on to the next project. Now we'll show you how to read the state of a Consumidor using one of the analog inputs.

ANALOG INPUT WITH A POTENTIOMETER

Hi. In this project, I'm going to show you how to take readings from a potentiometer like this one here, a rotary potentiometer or other. I don't look at devices such as a photoresistor, for example, using the ESP three to analog to digital. And to begin with, just want to have a quick look at the documentation that is provided. This tutorial up here and we can learn that the specific tube contains a number of the digital converters that provides us with will beat resolution and could see total of 18 channels measurement channels and we have the ATC one which contains eight channels attached to GPIO 7239 and then a DC two which contains an additional ten channels in those GPIO. And I'll show you the pin map in a second. Is there anything to remember about all these? Is that the second ADC? ADC two is restrictions that have to do with the usage of ADC to by the Wi-Fi driver.

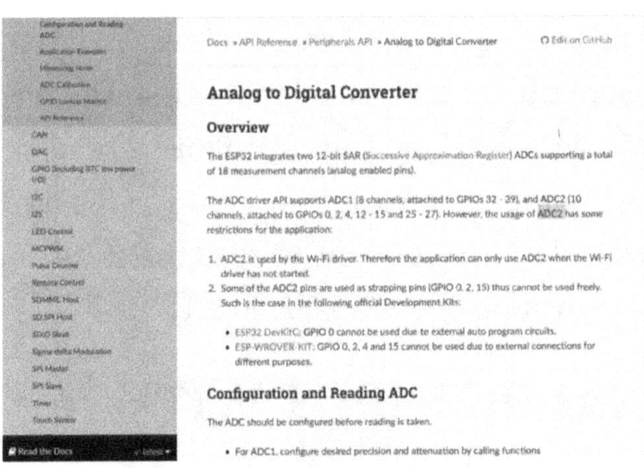

So what that means, let's look at them. If you will. We're going to do the experiment. So here's a map with ADC one and then ADC two In this view, over here, ten in total for ADC to the ADC, two pins can be used or channels I should say can be used when the Wi-Fi is not running.

Otherwise we are restricted to using ADC one. So in this experiment I'm just going to show you the simplest possible experiment. Are we using a potentiometer? We use one of the ADC ones to just take more readings from the potentiometer and show them on the serial monitor. And then in the next project, I'll show you how to convert those readings to heat and values and drive in sleep using those values. So here's the example circuit very simple. We go to a ten ohm rotary potentiometer that is connected PIN number 1 to 3.3 votes. PIN number three or number two. In this diagram, it's connected to ground. So here's the ground. Here is number one. It goes to three points, people. And then we take the readings from the middle pin W, which goes to pin number three in this diagram, which is GPIO three six here in a pin map.

Now have a look at these kids. It is running on the HP 32. Very simple. We first define the GPIO PWD to which we have connected the signal in the partition. We initialize the serial ward and the setup function so we can take readings out of it. And then in the loop we constantly take readings on that GPIO using an input create, which is a function that we can live with from the TRINO. Let's absolutely sketch and come to hold the boot button to put the data into a plug mode. Okay, done. And bring up the serial one itself and extend the numbers. All right. So about halfway through and here, move it all the way to the other end counterclockwise. And I reach the maximum 4095, which is the number of steps in the twin feet resolution. And I look, the digital converter reminds you that the do not you know we see the 328 is coordinated with the resolution. We go. So that's how easy it is to use a potentiometer or other analog devices. As I said earlier, such as a flicker system or a touch potentiometer like a patch since the potentiometer with your ISP 32. Now let's take this circuit one step further in the next project where I'll connect an LCD to that. Use 52 and then use W enter to drive the brightness of the reality as I turn the potentiometer.

ANALOG INPUT WITH POTENTIOMETER AND PWM OUTPUT

Hi. In this project, we are going to build on the example from the previous project in which you learned how to use a consumer with your ISP. Three to to drive led using p w m. So we're simply going to take the output from the analog to digital converter and then send it off to the LDC right function so we can control the intensity or the brightness of reality. To do this is very easy. All we have to do is to combine the two sketches that we've seen in previous projects. The one is from the previous project, 50, where you learn that you can use the analog read function to read the state of the potentiometer. And a little bit earlier in project 20, in section four, you learned about how to use the DC write function in order to pass a pickup new value to a particular digital to analog channel that is attached to a particular GPIO. So kind of put these two away and show you when you switch it looks like this. I've got the potentiometer connected to GPIO 36 which got the LTE connected to GPIO 32 We don't really need the brightness and fader mount functions, so I'll just delete them then in setup we attach Channel zero to entity GPO, which is 32 using LDC, attach PIN, and then we set this channel to a 12 bit resolution.

```
 * 1. ledc.h source code: https://github.com/espressif/arduino-esp32/blob/
 * 2. ESP32 Datasheet: https://www.espressif.com/sites/default/files/docum
 *
 * Created on March 27 2019 by Peter Dalmaris
 *
 */

const byte POT_GPIO = 36; // Potentiometer
const byte led_gpio = 32; // the PWM pin the LED is attached to
int brightness = 0;      // how bright the LED is
int fadeAmount = 5;      // how many points to fade the LED by

// the setup routine runs once when you press reset:
void setup() {
  ledcAttachPin(led_gpio, 0); // assign a led pins to a channel

  // Initialize channels
  // channels 0-15, resolution 1-16 bits, freq limits depend on resolution
  // ledcSetup(uint8_t channel, uint32_t freq, uint8_t resolution_bits);
  ledcSetup(0, 4000, 12); // 12 kHz PWM, 8-bit resolution
}

// the loop routine runs over and over again forever:
void loop() {
  ledcWrite(0, analogRead(POT_GPIO)); // set the brightness of the LED

}
```

```
Hard resetting via RTS pin...
/Volumes/GoogleDrive/Team Drives/Courses/ESP32 For Busy People/Git/04-020_Digi
```

You can set it to other resolutions like from 1 to 16 bits, but you may remember from the previous project that the analog read function in the ESP 32is called the Resolution of 12. So I decided to make the P.W in resolution also 12. In this way, we don't need to use the mapping function to convert the 12 bits of the analog to digital converter to a different number of bits for the P.W. And that is, I just remind you that if you choose something else for example, if you choose eight, then you will need to use the map function, which works the same way as India does in the world. All right, so let's put this back to 12. And in the book we call the DC write function. We pass the converter channel that we want zero, which is attached to GPIO 36, and then we call the analog read function to take a reading from the potential error. Before we upload the sketch, let's have a look at the wiring as well. So I've got the potentiometer connected, just like in the previous project. Two chips here, 36 via the orange wire, and then we've got the LCD, I've got the anode show. The long pin is connected to GP Arrow 32, this one right here. And then via the current limiting resistor goes to ground. So let's go ahead and upload the circuit. You hold down the boot button to get my ESP32 into upload mode.

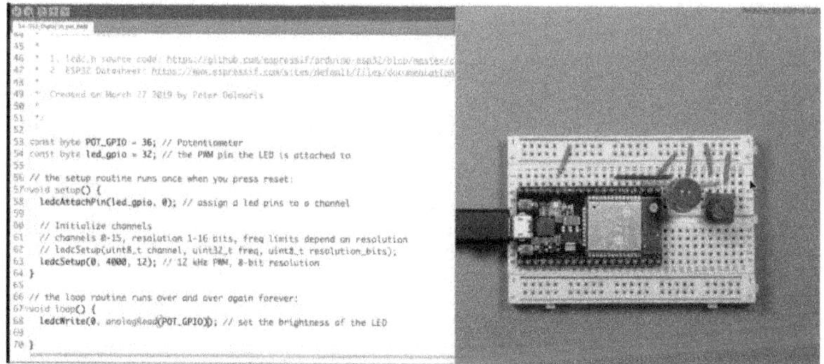

Okay, we can turn the knob counterclockwise and the intensity of the media is increasing and counterclockwise. The intensity is decreasing easily. All right. So this is how you can use pwm with your analog digital converter taking readings from the potentiometer. Now in the next project, I'm going to show you how you can actually use the potentiometer instead of adding pwm values to actually control the voltage that comes out of a digital to analog converter pin. So what I'm saying is that instead of controlling the duty cycle of P.W Antonucci coming out of an area, we actually control the voltage because the DSP 32 has got a real digital to analog converter and it can output voltage, can drive any Lety or whatever else you want to drive from the analog to digital converter pins, and that's a lot of them as well. So let's have a look at that in the next project.

AN OVERVIEW OF DIGITAL TO ANALOG CONVERSION IN THE ESP32

Hi. In the previous project, you learned how you can use your ESP three to to create an approximation of an analog output signal using Sigma delta modulation. In addition to what you've learned earlier about post with modulation signals both paid to him and Sigma Delta modulated signals and not true analog signals, they are approximations. The HP Theory two does have the hardware necessary to create true analog output signals, and in this project I'll show you how to use that capability. So in this project here, you had to create a true analytic signal using the available two digital, two analog converters in the ESP 32. So we'll create a variety of signals, see them on the oscilloscope, and also make some sounds using those signals using a piece of sound. Before we start with the experiment, let's have a look at the DSP 32 programing guide.

Some useful information here. The URL to this guide is available in the example sketch. You can go up here and you'll find the source for the data sheet and a few other things here as well. So what we learned is that the ease with Rita has got to eight bit digital to analog converter channels, and those are connected to GPI. 25, which is Channel one and GPIO 26, which is Channel two, and we can take a look at the map and learn that there's two digital, two analog converters here. So it's called the AC one connected to IO 25 and the digital converter which is connected to GPIO 26. In my experiment here, I connected the orange wire, just escaped it from the GPIO leaf. It is 25, which is a DC one.

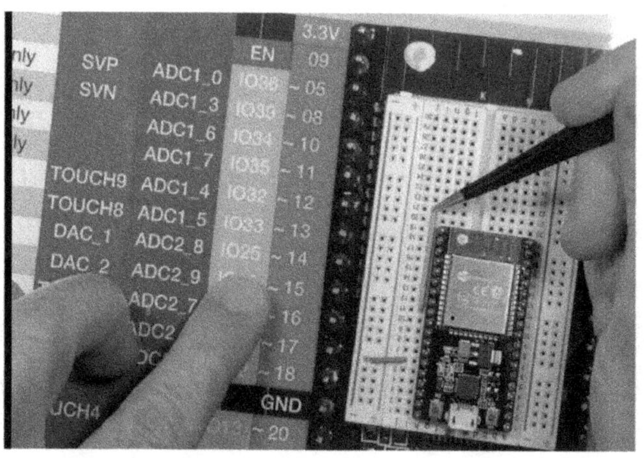

So this chip IO 25 and this is where I connect my oscilloscope. And later on that buzzer back in data alimentation. Let's see what else is interesting. If you go to the technical reference menu and search for this section 28.5 to see if you also learned would go to a bit back channel. These are totally independent. The voltage you can create any voltage between zero and the voltage reference that is connected in the d3p3dc pin, which is not exposed in the prototyping module. I just connected internally to the power supply. Practically, this means that the digital to analog converter can produce a voltage in its two channels that goes from zero to about 3.3, since that is the voltage of operation of the USB three to.

DAC DEMO SKETCH

Let's take a look at the sketch. Here's a sketch for the example. And what I've got here is just a few different waveforms. This first one here is very simple. It will just raise the voltage on the output pin from zero volts, which of course points to values 0 to 3.3 volts should be that which corresponds to value 255. And would you say DAC is the right function for that? In the right function we need to provide the period which we want to use and it's going to be 25 or 26 and then the eight bit value from 0 to 255. So in the first for loop, I'm producing a rising slope from zero votes to 3.3 volts and in the second loop the voltage drops. So from 255 or 3.3 volts approximately And again, I'm using DAC right to produce that in the output signal. And then I'm going to show you some other examples of sine wave signals. And that square signal in a triangle, the signal which is actually calculated on the fly using a little bit of trigonometry.

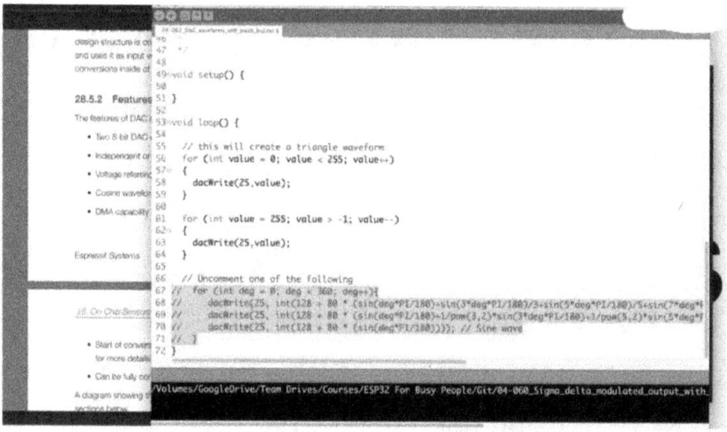

So if you are familiar with trigonometric functions this is going to make sense, but we'll see what the outcome is anyway. So all you've got to remember to do is you can generate any kind of wave for any kind of voltage output in the AC channels by either writing a value directly in DAC, right. Or creating a formula that will generate the function. If you have studied, have my other course Advanced Adreno Boards and tools. I've got a project here that shows you how you can actually use calculators that can generate arbitrary waveform sets. You can store in an array and then produce and call and write to the digital analog converter. So if you're interested in learning more about this topic, have a look at this project.

DAC ANALOG WAVEFORM DEMO

Before we go and try out this sketch, I want to have a look at the right function. The pedophile for these functions here slowing down causes SB three to look at the SB three to see in my case on the Mac OS this file is right it see here so this file here which for the Mac is under the library folder and here is the hierarchy. So this is where the idea is stored. Code I do with 15 packages is P 32 hardware is pathetic to the version cause it's P and in here you've got all of the files that make up the PSP. 3 to 4 support. And one of those is that H which is this file here. So here we learn that the back right function requires an eight bit number for the GPIO and an eight bit number for the value. Very simple. All right. So let's begin a first experiment with just this simple waveform. It's just going to be a triangle. Try Angular, I should say waveform going up and then going down and then repeating. And that's why I think of an oscilloscope so we can see it first. I'm going to plug in the ground and then from here, the blue channel, except history oriented cameras, turn on the oscilloscope. And while that is happening, we're going to upload the sketch with the okay, so we only need the first channel on the scope.

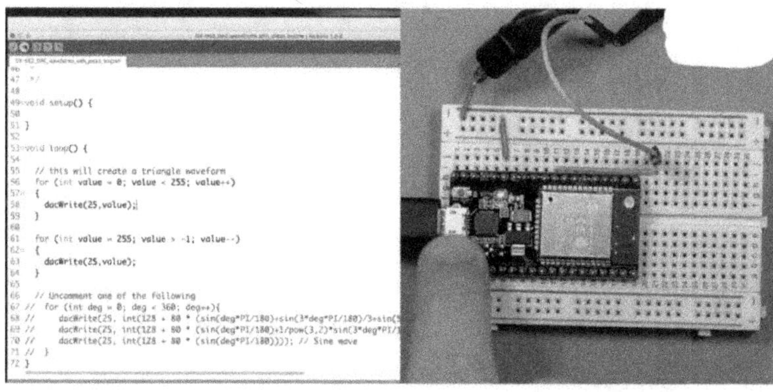
void setup() {
}
void loop() {
// this will create a triangle waveform
for (int value = 0; value < 255; value++)
{
dacWrite(25,value);
}
for (int value = 255; value > -1; value--)
{
dacWrite(25,value);
}
// Uncomment one of the following
// for (int deg = 0; deg < 360; deg++){
// dacWrite(25, int(128 + 80 * (sin(deg*PI/180)+sin(3*deg*PI/180)/3+
// dacWrite(25, int(128 + 80 * (sin(deg*PI/180)+1/pow(3,2)*
// dacWrite(25, int(128 + 80 * (sin(deg*PI/180)))); // Sine wave
// }
}

Let's have a look at what the waveform is. Now you care. Sorry, sir. Away from that is composed by a rising voltage, then a dropping voltage. Let's check out the other two way forms. So I'm going to comment out the first part of the sketch and then uncomment the loop and let's go for a sine wave. So I'm going to comment on the last line and the sine wave is calculated using this formula. So here we don't have a 0 to 255 value. We are counting decrease here because this input formula uses degrees to convert those degrees into a value from 0 to 255.

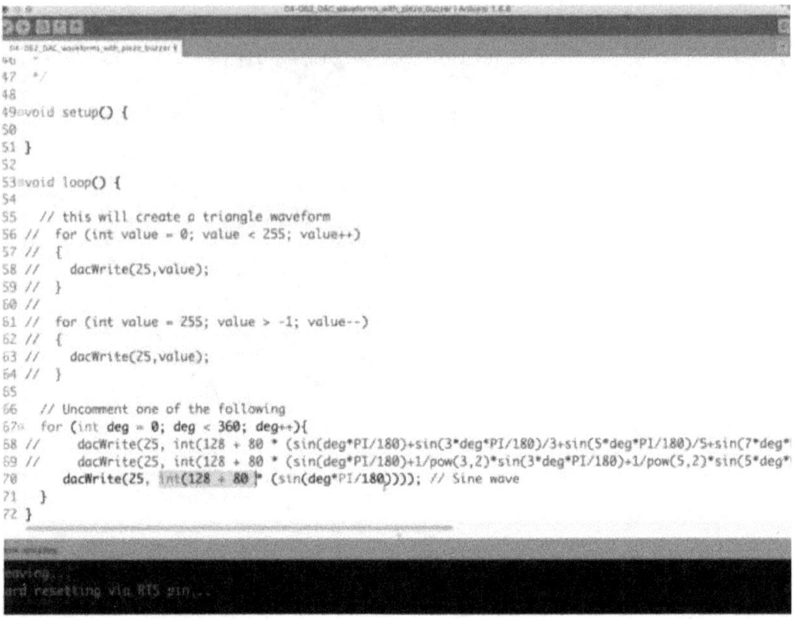

```
 */

void setup() {

}

void loop() {

  // this will create a triangle waveform
//  for (int value = 0; value < 255; value++)
//  {
//    dacWrite(25,value);
//  }
//
//  for (int value = 255; value > -1; value--)
//  {
//    dacWrite(25,value);
//  }

  // Uncomment one of the following
  for (int deg = 0; deg < 360; deg++){
//     dacWrite(25, int(128 + 80 * (sin(deg*PI/180)+sin(3*deg*PI/180)/3+sin(5*deg*PI/180)/5+sin(7*deg*
//     dacWrite(25, int(128 + 80 * (sin(deg*PI/180)+1/pow(3,2)*sin(3*deg*PI/180)+1/pow(5,2)*sin(5*deg*
     dacWrite(25, int(128 + 80 * (sin(deg*PI/180)))); // Sine wave
  }
}
```

```
aving...
rd resetting via RTS pin...
```

Okay. That and there is our sine wave. So let's try out another one, maybe a square wave and see what the square wave looks like. This one here is a square wave comment and absolute pitch. You can see the square wave is not perfect, which is called harmonics or distortion up the top and the bottom of the wave. And this because we're using trigonometry to try and approximate it. We could do a much better job if we just used that right to write that 255 value for as long as we want the signal to be high and a zero value for as long as you want the signal to be zero. And the edges, of course, will be sharp, nice up and down without these harmonics. But this is just an example of what you can do with a bit of trigonometry. And as a last example, let's have a look at just kind of coming this out and the last one is a triangle. So I've already created a triangle up here and with my two loops, but let's try and use again this trigonometric function to see what a triangular waveform would look like using this method. So I'm trying to sketch and there you go. It's not exactly a triangle. It looks more like a sine wave, but it's got more rounded edges up the top and the bottom than a sine wave. Good. So this is another example. So they can come up with various functions here. Or as I said earlier, you can use calculators, as I'm showing in this project in advance leaderboards and tools. I've got links to some calculators here that I can do, including this project in this project. So then you can use those to create tables of any kind from that you want to produce encoded into your ESPN 32 sketch.

MAKING NOISE WITH THE DAC

And before we complete this project, I'm going to unplug the oscilloscope and replace it with a simple piers or buzzer to show you how you can use a buzzer to create noise. So I'm going to plug the buzzer into the fretboard. I'm going to plug in one pin of the peer pressure to ground. I'm turning off the oscilloscope and using a jumper wire to connect the other pin to the output of the to the output of the digital analog converter. And let's upload a let's hear the sound to that. And this triangular signal makes sound and comments and uploads the sketch. And that is the sound of a triangular waveform. What about the sound of a sound wave? Right.

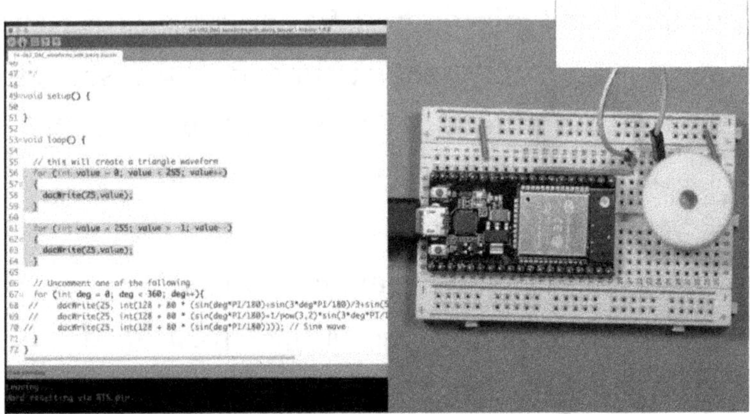
void setup() {
void loop() {
// this will create a triangle waveform
dacWrite(25,value);
dacWrite(25,value);
// Uncomment one of the following

So I still have my loop running and just uncommitted. Is this line here that produces a sine wave and is amplified? It's a very faint sound. I'm going to put it close to my microphone so you can hear it. Okay. And of course, this is not amplified. And that's why this sound doesn't sound. The volume of these bars isn't very loud. And we can try one more thing here. Can comment out the loop and try to make this sound a little bit more coarse. So instead of increasing the value by one in each loop, make it increase by five. So this makes it like this plus five. And then down here and it's going to be equal to the value minus five. See what the effect is on the sound that is produced.

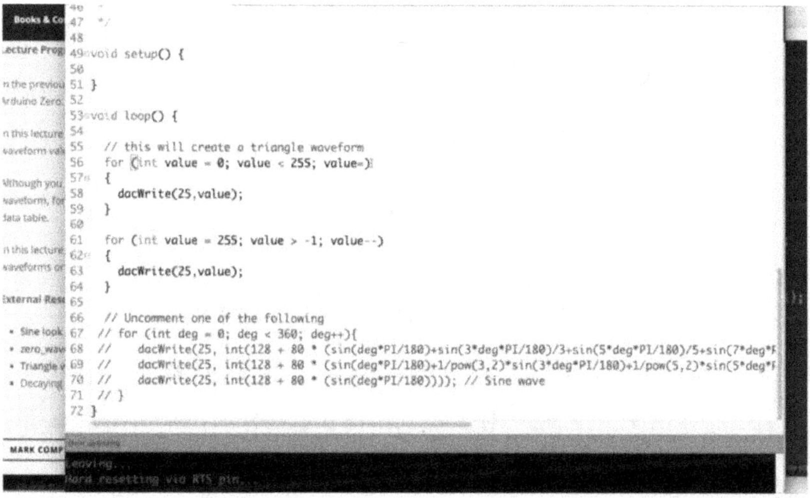

```
*/

void setup() {

}

void loop() {

  // this will create a triangle waveform
  for (int value = 0; value < 255; value++)
  {
    dacWrite(25,value);
  }

  for (int value = 255; value > -1; value--)
  {
    dacWrite(25,value);
  }

  // Uncomment one of the following
  // for (int deg = 0; deg < 360; deg++){
  //    dacWrite(25, int(128 + 80 * (sin(deg*PI/180)+sin(3*deg*PI/180)/3+sin(5*deg*PI/180)/5+sin(7*deg*F
  //    dacWrite(25, int(128 + 80 * (sin(deg*PI/180)+1/pow(3,2)*sin(3*deg*PI/180)+1/pow(5,2)*sin(5*deg*F
  //    dacWrite(25, int(128 + 80 * (sin(deg*PI/180)))); // Sine wave
  // }
}
```

```
Leaving...
Hard resetting via RTS pin...
```

Okay, This sounds like this. The higher pitched one region, you know, stops this noise. The main reason that I chose this sound just to produce a sound from these waveforms is because the buzzer takes very little current from the SB 32. So I did not need to use an amplifier for this test. You can actually try f larger speakers, but you would need to also include an amplifier if you do so because the ESP three two will not be able to produce enough current to drive a larger speaker. Have something like this. You need to play two or three. What amplifier? So this concludes this experiment. We are showing you how to use a digital in the next project, which is going to be the last for this section. I'm going to show you how to use a button. But this time, instead of constantly holding the button to reach each value, you would use an interrupt so that the power operation of the SPCA two will be interrupted when the button is pressed and then have an interrupt service routine to do something in response to the button press. So let's check that out next.

GPIO INTERRUPTS, AN INTRODUCTION

In a previous project, we used a circuit like the one that we're looking at here. It contains a pattern in an elite, and when a person patterns, the elite would come on. In that project we used a function, a digital read function inside the loop to read the state of the button and then control the ability. What we're doing this project is instead of doing this reading of the button state inside the loop to actually create an interrupt, connect the button to end interrupts, and then when the button is pressed, the interrupts face, it stops the hospitality from doing whatever else it might be doing at that point in time and take a reading of the button.

And then and then write a new value to the entity. So this is important because as much as possible, good programing practice is to not constantly pull for things like button states inside the main loop, but assign those things to interrupts in order to make more efficient use of the hardware. So that's what we'll do in this project in terms of the hardware and wiring thing, things are very simple. You've seen this before with quite a push button and that is connected to a chip area of 25 and you can attach interrupts on any type pro. So this one is attached to or 25, and then the other pin of the push button goes to ground. I chose not to use a pull up or pull down resistor in this example, and instead of that we'll use an internal pull up. I'll show you how to do that in code in a minute. And then for any day we've connected the anode via the resistor to IO 32 and the other end of the day and the resistor goes to ground. Let's have a look at the example sketch to learn how to implement interrupt driven programing in SB 32. It's very similar to what you would have done in the Arduino with the difference. It only has two pins that you can use to attach external interrupts to where this is no limitation in the ESP 32.

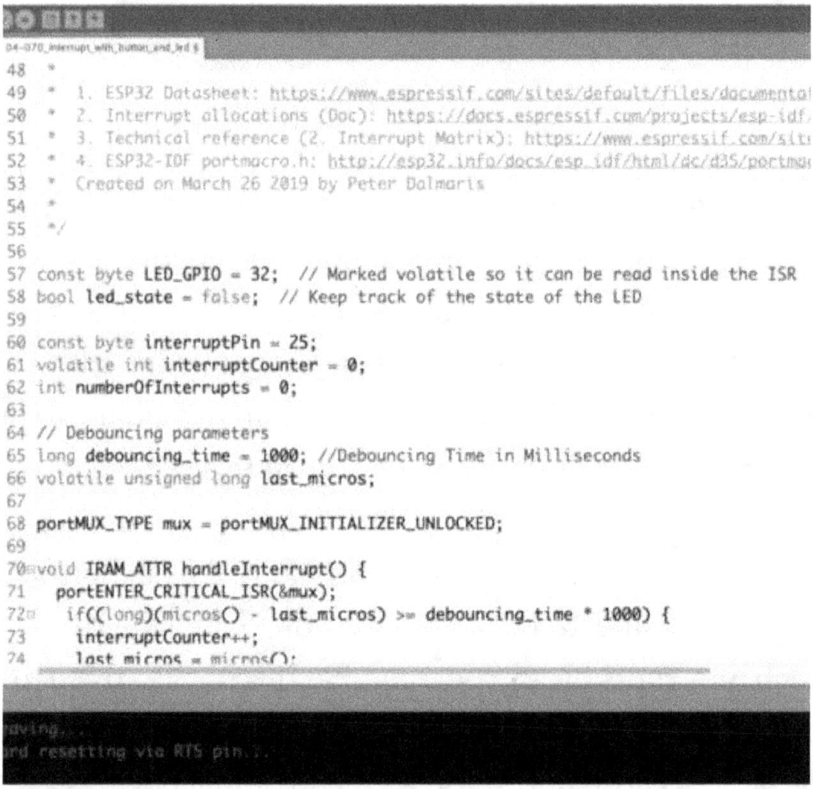

04-070_interrupt_with_button_and_led $
 *
 * 1. ESP32 Datasheet: https://www.espressif.com/sites/default/files/documenta
 * 2. Interrupt allocations (Doc): https://docs.espressif.com/projects/esp-idf
 * 3. Technical reference (2. Interrupt Matrix): https://www.espressif.com/sit
 * 4. ESP32-IDF portmacro.h: http://esp32.info/docs/esp_idf/html/dc/d35/portma
 * Created on March 26 2019 by Peter Dalmaris
 *
 */

const byte LED_GPIO = 32; // Marked volatile so it can be read inside the ISR
bool led_state = false; // Keep track of the state of the LED

const byte interruptPin = 25;
volatile int interruptCounter = 0;
int numberOfInterrupts = 0;

// Debouncing parameters
long debouncing_time = 1000; //Debouncing Time in Milliseconds
volatile unsigned long last_micros;

portMUX_TYPE mux = portMUX_INITIALIZER_UNLOCKED;

void IRAM_ATTR handleInterrupt() {
  portENTER_CRITICAL_ISR(&mux);
  if((long)(micros() - last_micros) >= debouncing_time * 1000) {
    interruptCounter++;
    last_micros = micros();
aving...
rd resetting via RTS pin...

So here's the sketch and here I've got further reading that I encourage you to do. An interesting reading is the interrupt allocation. The link for that is this one here. So here you can learn about the way that interrupts have been implemented in SB 32. As you know, the SB three two has got two cores and each of those cores has 32 interrupts at various protein levels. And there's a lot of details here that are useful to know. I'm going to leave this up to you to read. And another one is the technical reference. So this is this document here. Just jump to section two, interrupt matrix. It's this one here. It shows you again how interrupts built in these P 32. So if caught on up 71 peripheral interrupt sources and inputs in what's called 26 peripheral interrupt sources passively, you etc.. It's a lot of details here. I'm going to come back to this document later and in particular this header file, because you will be using the attach interrupt function, you know, sketch. So I'll keep this handy and open for the time being.

GPIO INTERRUPTS, SKETCH AND DEMONSTRATION

Back to the example sketch and let's see what's happening. First, I set up the bios for the entity. I also have a variable here to remember the last state of the entity, because unlike the previous example, what I wanted to see was edited to remember the state in between button presses. But that's what this is. State boolean variable. It's got a variable here for the interrupt pin. That is a pin that the button is connected to. So this GPIO 25 and I could have used any of the GPIO. I went to count how many interrupts have been produced by pressing the button. So I've got an interrupt counter here. Initialize it to zero and I've also marked it as volatile because I want to be able to use this variable from inside it. The interrupt request handling routine. So this is a special function. Insert this function. I've got code that deals with the interrupt, as you can see. And what I do is to increase the increment in the value stored in the interrupt counter variable.

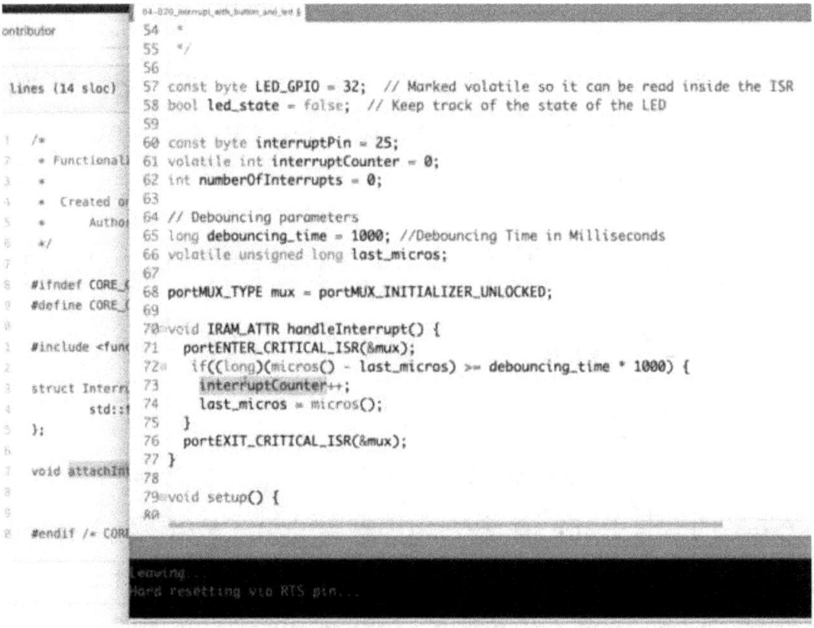

```
 *
 */

const byte LED_GPIO = 32;  // Marked volatile so it can be read inside the ISR
bool led_state = false;  // Keep track of the state of the LED

const byte interruptPin = 25;
volatile int interruptCounter = 0;
int numberOfInterrupts = 0;

// Debouncing parameters
long debouncing_time = 1000; //Debouncing Time in Milliseconds
volatile unsigned long last_micros;

portMUX_TYPE mux = portMUX_INITIALIZER_UNLOCKED;

void IRAM_ATTR handleInterrupt() {
  portENTER_CRITICAL_ISR(&mux);
   if((long)(micros() - last_micros) >= debouncing_time * 1000) {
    interruptCounter++;
    last_micros = micros();
   }
  portEXIT_CRITICAL_ISR(&mux);
}

void setup() {
```

And for this variable to be accessible and modifiable from inside this interrupt handling routine, I need to market as volatile. I also got another variable called the number of interrupts. This is just the cumulative number of button presses which produced interrupt requests so that I can write that number in the serial monitor CAC in a minute. So I'm going to skip this part of the code for a second. We're going to come back to it a little bit later, and I want to have a look inside the setup just to see how the interrupt assignment is made in the setup. First, I set up the serial monitor so I can get it, so I can see the number of interrupt messages that are coming out of the program. I've got my ability to be here set to be output. Sending a message then goes out to the monitor, the interrupt pin. I set it up here with an input pull up resistor and internal input pull up resistor instead of having an external resistor connected on the breadboard. And finally, this is where I'm actually attaching this pin to the interrupt you say attach interrupt function, which is defined here in the or the noise P3 to core function or interrupt. Don't hedge the header file. And it's this function here that sends an eight bit number for the pin to interrupt.

```
/*
 * FunctionalInterrupt.h
 *
 *  Created on: 8 jul. 2018
 *      Author: Herman
 */

#ifndef CORE_CORE_FUNCTIONALINTERRUPT_H_
#define CORE_CORE_FUNCTIONALINTERRUPT_H_

#include <functional>

struct InterruptArgStructure {
	std::function<void(void)> interruptFunction;
};

void attachInterrupt(uint8_t pin, std::function<void(void)> intRoutine, int mode);


#endif /* CORE_CORE_FUNCTIONALINTERRUPT_H_ */
```

So this routine function and then the mode of the interrupt. So I have programmed this interrupt to trigger when I depress the button. Sort of got the second pane of the button connected to ground. So when I when a person then I let go of the button, there's just a falling edge and this is what's going to trigger the interrupt for the interrupt handling routine for French, the handle interrupt function, which is defined up here. So this is in the handle interrupt function. This subtype I ran underscore edge. So it's an interruption. So this routine and what happens in here is that the first thing that I do is to mark the segment of the code between this function and in this function as the critical section.

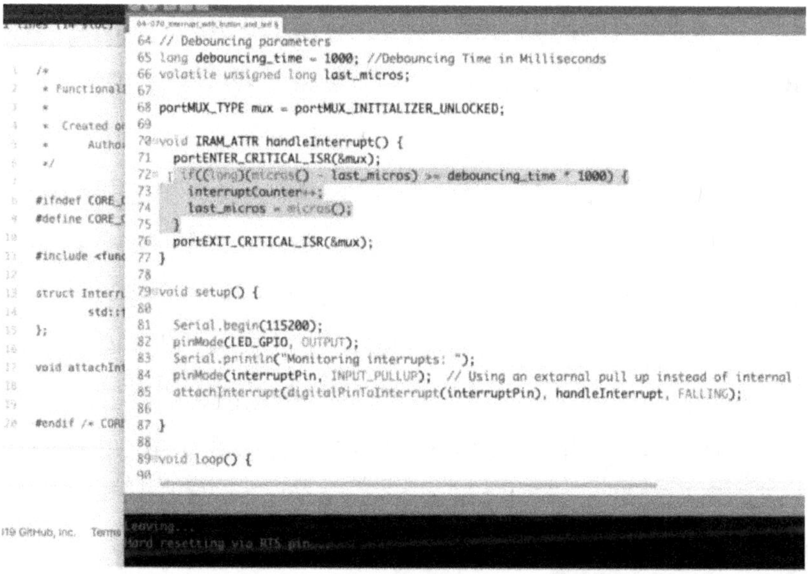

```
// Debouncing parameters
long debouncing_time = 1000; //Debouncing Time in Milliseconds
volatile unsigned long last_micros;

portMUX_TYPE mux = portMUX_INITIALIZER_UNLOCKED;

void IRAM_ATTR handleInterrupt() {
  portENTER_CRITICAL_ISR(&mux);
  if((long)(micros() - last_micros) >= debouncing_time * 1000) {
    interruptCounter++;
    last_micros = micros();
  }
  portEXIT_CRITICAL_ISR(&mux);
}

void setup() {

  Serial.begin(115200);
  pinMode(LED_GPIO, OUTPUT);
  Serial.println("Monitoring interrupts: ");
  pinMode(interruptPin, INPUT_PULLUP);  // Using an extornal pull up instead of internal
  attachInterrupt(digitalPinToInterrupt(interruptPin), handleInterrupt, FALLING);

}

void loop() {
```

```
Leaving...
Hard resetting via RTS pin...
```

So while these lines of code are executed, all the interrupts on the HP thread two are disabled. So that I can't interrupt and interrupt. So we call this the critical section, and I'm making a reference to this special macro. This is a macro called port, and you X underscore initialize, underscore unlocked, which I believe is referenced somewhere here and go. So it's under ESP three two I.D.s and this is the port microdot page file where these macros are referenced and searched for. You'll find its definition here. I'm not going to go into the details of what it is, but if you're interested to know exactly how this macro works and can investigate further. But for the purposes of this demonstration, this is not within right now. I've got the URL to this file right here. It's number four to check it out. If you want to know the details. So watch what happens once you go into the critical segment. First we check to see if we had an interrupt within the particular bouncing amount of time. So because you want to make sure that we don't get false triggers of the button press because it's a mechanical electrical device. When you press it, you can cause bouncing triggers of this interrupt. So it can have within a single physical press, they can have dozens and dozens of actual interrupt calls. And I want to clear all that up by introducing a bit of good bouncing code. And that's what this is doing here. So I'm saying that I want to only accept a single interrupt request every second. So this is the number of the bouncing time in milliseconds. So that gives us a second. So I'm saying that I'm not going to be pressing this button faster than once per second and any in between presses. So any presses within an amount of time, less than a thousand milliseconds should be ignored. And that's what happens here. I'm ignoring anything. Any button presses that are happening within 1000 milliseconds. But if more than a second has elapsed since the last time the button was pressed or the last time that the interrupt to retain was triggered, then go inside the block, inside the if statement and increase the interrupt counter by one. Then take the new last micros a new time that will count towards the next time that we evaluate this statement. So this is a classic way to implement software bouncing with patterns. So once this is finished with code here in incremented interrupt counter the plus plus. So from zero, the original value of this counter we go to one. So then it takes us to the loop in the loop, constantly going around and then we check once per loop whether the interrupt counter is larger than zero. If we have just exited the interrupt service routine, then interrupt count would contain the value one which is larger than zero. So that would take us inside this block. And again, you can see that we are defining a critical segment in our program that we are calling Port and the critical referencing the you x macro, which we defined up here. So we mark whatever follows as a critical section to not be interrupted. We reduce the value interrupt counter. So from one we make it zero and then we mark the end of the critical section. We are still in the if statement. So then we'll turn the on and switch the state of the state variable and increase the number of interrupts variable to the new number and print it out in a monitor. So take this time to go through this a couple of times to make sure that you understand the logic and how it works. But once you have it, it will make the switch. Go ahead and upload the sketch and see it in action.

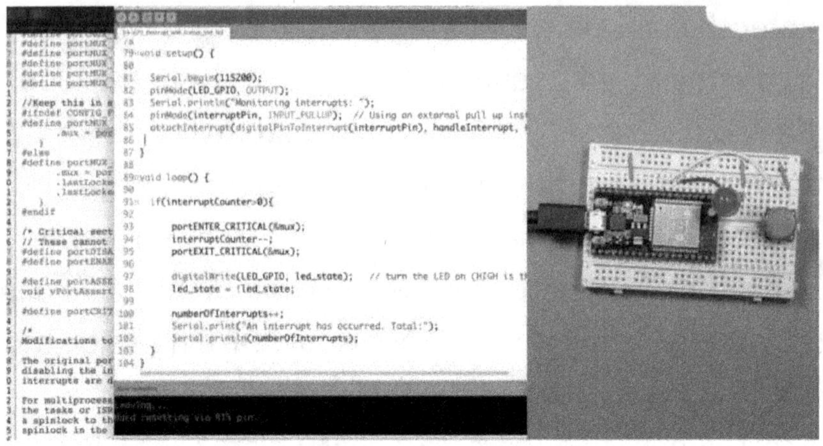

All right. Uploaded. I'm going to bring up the serial monitor and press the button. So this first interrupt the needs of another, interrupt the notice on total interrupts to just one more time. Turn it off track Couple of fast presses Say only one of those counted again. Okay, only one counted again. So you can see how the bouncing code in software works. So we have no bouncing clear signal on the end of the case. So I hope this makes sense and time. You now have a better understanding of how interrupts work in the HP 32 and with this project we conclude the projects in this section of the course. In the next section, we'll continue the course with our review of several sensors, some of which are actually integrated into the HP three two so you don't have to connect anything external. And once we have a look at those internal sensors, integrated sensors, we'll plug in a few external ones.

INTEGRATED HALL EFFECT (USE A MAGNET)

Hi. This is the first project in this section about census and how to use your various ID such with your ISP. 32 And the first sensor that I want to show you how to use is actually integrated inside his p32. And it's a sensor that allows you to detect magnetic fields. So what I've got here is a magnet that I'm putting close to. So placing it close to the sensor, then I'm going to get a reading indicating the presence of the magnet by this sensor. And this is a whole effect sensor and it's called a hall effect. And what effect is the effect that a magnet has on the sensor? If you want to learn more about the hall effect sensor, I recommend this Wikipedia article. It explains the physics behind how this particular sensor works. You can also connect an external hall effect since you look at the map of the pins.

So on the SB 32, you've got these two pins dedicated to connecting an external hall effect. These two pins contain amplifiers that can amplify the weak signal that this sensor produces in order for it to be able to be used and translated by the analog to digital converter inside the P32. But in this example, we'll just go with the building sensor. So let's have a quick look at the sketch. There's nothing to connect, obviously, since we are going to be using only the internal components. Here is a sketch at the there is no external library to use and install and will be using just a code or the will be using the functions that come with the doing, not ISP or installation. So here we've got a variable, just an integer that we used to store the value that we get from the sensor. He and the set up method will just initialize the serial monitor at 9600 ports and then inside the loop we use the whole read function to get a reading from the integrated whole sensor and then print it out.

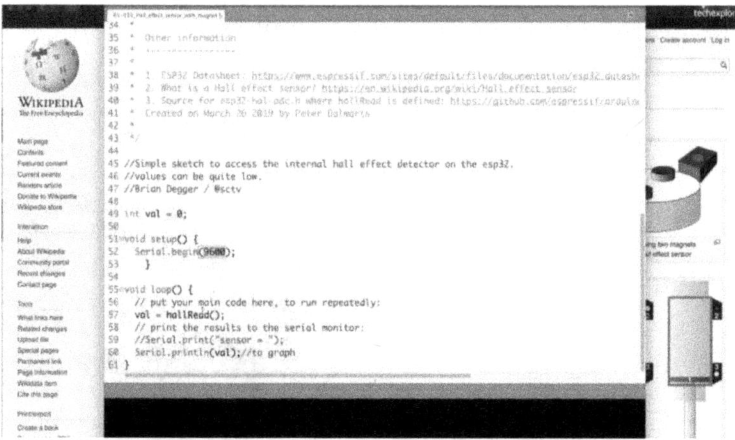

So this particular function, you can have a look at it in the source code here in this file, which is the one of the five that come, we see the HP three to or and if you look at it, it's a CSP three to how it is. See the page hit a file somewhere down here. There we use the whole read function to return a picture and that's all there is. Just read it. So let's try it out. I'll connect the speaker to my computer via a USB to get the cable to stay put. Okay. And upload the sketch and hold onto the boot button to enable the output mood on the ISP. 32. All right. Now let's bring up the serial monitor. You can see a bunch of numbers coming through. You can take them a magnet and just place it over the sensor for the sensation around here to place the magnet on it. They get a different number there. I'm going to put it close so I can see that number increases for switching the magnet over, to get the opposite magnetic field. Then the number becomes positive.

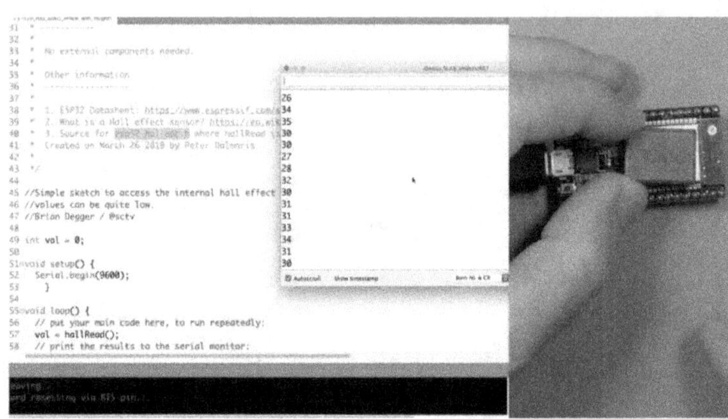

So the number that you see in the serial monitor depends on the strength of the magnetic field that the magnet produces. Something else. I've got a really powerful magnet that I got out of a hard disk. So this is a magnet here, and it's much stronger than this one here. So let's see what we get out of it. Can you place it right over? It's stuck on the edge without it. You can see it's gone up to two hundredths. Flip it over. The other side is not as powerful. It's probably because of the metal that is attached to the magnet. So they go, yes, pretty simple. Probably. I manipulate the cable too much. I'm going to stick it in Bitcoin and restart the serial port shrink in a bit. More generally, this time, it's a really strong magnet. All right, here you go. Much larger values now. And of course, we are printing only a single value. I should also be able to use the serial plotter tool and actually visualize that graph, the density of this magnetic field so used that we can magnetize again and you can see how that changes. You can turn it over. Okay, Positive values. And I use a stronger hard disk mechanism. You get much stronger values. They get all much smaller negative values depending on the orientation. So how you go, that's how you can use your SB 32 and it's integrated whole since simple to think sensor to detect and to measure magnetic fields.

TOUCH (CAPACITIVE) SENSOR WITH LED

Hi. In the previous project, you learned how to use the integrated whole effect sensor. That's a sensor. It allows you to detect and measure magnetic fields. In this project and the next one, I'll show you how to use another integrated sensor to the speaker to the touch sensor. With a touch sensor, you can do something like this or cut a jumper while I am just exposed connected to a digital pin. And which one is it? One, two, three, four, five, four. Digital pin 13 which is one of the available touch GPIO enabled sensors. And just by touching the tip of this temple wire, the entity is activated. So this is a touch sensor. Can I show you how to use a touch sensor in this?

And then in the next project, I'm going to show you how to use it a bit more efficiently using external chips, IO interrupts.

Let's have a look at the wiring first. What I've got here is the three to have just a single wire connected to one of the available to use that have a touch sense capability. And again, having a look at the map pin map, we learn that you can connect wire for the purposes of using it as a touch sensor in any of the areas that are marked as touch or touch four, five, six, seven, eight, nine and on the other side we've got another four, three, two, one zero. So any of those you can use is a touch sensor that controls that in order to visualize the effect of that touch.

Since I've got an LCD, every time I touch the wire, the entity comes on and I've connected this entity to it, said Chip IO 32 right here via a current and meeting the resistance to ground. This is around $300. So that's all there is to it. Let's have a look at a sketch. So here's a sketch and I've got some documentation here for the code that implements touch functionality and that just shows you the source code is right here. So we are looking at not using P core files. One of those files is the touch page. In here you'll find the touch read function. This returns a to byte number of an integer, and the closer that this number is to zero there, the stronger the touch is. I'll show you how that number changes in a minute in the next project, which is going to show you how to attach a touch sensor pin to an interrupt to show that you don't have to check the state of the sensor inside the boot.

```
 * accuracy depend on these values. Defaults are
 * 0x1000 for measure and 0x1000 for sleep.
 * With default values touchRead takes 0.5ms
 * */
void touchSetCycles(uint16_t measure, uint16_t sleep);

/*
 * Read touch pad (values close to 0 mean touch detected)
 * You can use this method to chose a good threshold value
 * to use as value for touchAttachInterrupt
 * */
uint16_t touchRead(uint8_t pin);

/*
 * Set function to be called if touch pad value falls
 * below the given threshold. Use touchRead to determine
 * a proper threshold between touched and untouched state
 * */
void touchAttachInterrupt(uint8_t pin, void (*userFunc)(void), uint16_t threshold);

#ifdef __cplusplus
}
#endif

#endif /* MAIN_ESP32_HAL_TOUCH_H_ */
```

Just continue with a sketch. So define the GPO over which the LCD is connected. Then in set up, turn the area to output. Set up this serial monitor and at a delay just to wait for the ceremony to come up and print out your message and all that work, of course, happens inside the loop where we use the touch read function. A past the mnemonic name for the touch sensor that I'm using, which, as I said, it's touch for go in a print out this value to the serial monitor. Then experimentally I discovered that any value in the touch sensor below 20 indicates that I have touched the sensor and that it becomes smaller the more contact that my finger comes with the pin. So if I just touch the tip, I get a value that is very close to 20. And then if I touch the whole length of the pin, that value becomes closer to zero. And if it is closer to zero, then I'll turn the LCD on. Otherwise I'll turn it off and then wait for 500 milliseconds and try again. In the next project.

```
 *  1. ESP32 Datasheet: https://www.espressif.com/sites/default/files/documentatic
 *  2. esp32-hal-touch.h: https://github.com/espressif/arduino-esp32/blob/master/c
 *
 *  Created on March 27 2019 by Peter Dalmaris
 *
 */

const byte LED_GPIO = 32;  // Marked volatile so it can be read inside the ISR

void setup()
{
  pinMode(LED_GPIO, OUTPUT);
  Serial.begin(115200);
  delay(1000); // give me time to bring up serial monitor
  Serial.println("ESP32 Touch Test");
}

void loop()
{
  Serial.println(touchRead(T4));  // get value using T4

  if (touchRead(T4) < 20)         // The value 20 is determined experimentally
    digitalWrite(LED_GPIO, HIGH);
  else
    digitalWrite(LED_GPIO, LOW);

  delay(500);
}
```

I'll show you how to avoid using the delay function here and just use an interrupt in order to improve the efficiency of this code. But to keep things simple with the first example of using the delay function. So let's upload the sketch and have a look at the serial monitor and press the boot button to get my ESP module to update mode. Okay, let's bring up the serial monitor and change the speed of the communication to 1.5 200 points. All right. So that's the current value. I'm not touching the sensor and it said 77. Let's touch the tip. You can see the values eight and six, quite small. If I make more contact with a pen across its whole length, it drops down to three or five, gets closer to zero four. Hold it with my two fingers steady four. So that's another indication of another way of detecting the pressure of the air or the amount of contact during a touch event. Before we move on to the next project where I can show you how to implement the same functionality using the interrupt, it's a more efficient way of doing this. I want to show you how you can use this serial plotter instead of the serial monitor to visualize the touch events. Some can close the serial monitor, go to the original tools, and then bring up the plural and the plot of running. Can you touch the tip with my finger? All right, so you can see that the value has decreased. Let it go. It goes up again. Touch the graph drops, release graph goes up again and so on. So you can see that now, visually we can see that when I activate the touch sensor they graph groups. That's another way of saying this touch isn't great. Now let's move on to the next project where I'll show you how to achieve the same thing. But now using interrupts and avoiding having to use a delay inside to do so, we achieve the same thing, but a lot more efficiently and keep this method of the interrupts in mind because we'll be using it again later in this section with a couple of other experiments.

TOUCH (CAPACITIVE) SENSOR WITH INTERRUPTS AND LED

Hi. In the previous project, I showed you how to use the integrated Touch sensor in order to control and activate and be. We did that using the inefficient method that included having a delay inside the main loop. In this project, I'll show you how to do the exact same thing. But instead of using a delay in the loop, we'll interrupt a service routine which is a lot more efficient. Makes better use of the available hardware. So first, before I actually have a look at the code, I'm going to upload the sketch to show you how it works. So there's the updated sketch pressing the boot button to put my return to upload mode. Okay, it's done. So let's see, does it work? Okay, let's try this again. So I'm going to upload a sketch, hold down the boot button to get in the mood. So uploading and resetting. All right. So should the touch and the ability go on there, same functionality as before.

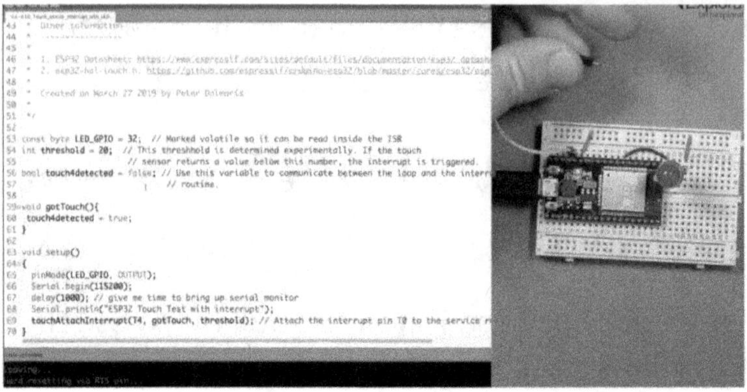

I've set it to stay on for half a second after each touch event. All right. Now the way this works is that I've used the touch attach interrupt function that is available in the ESP three to how Touch had a file. So what this function does is that it accepts the pin number to which the wire is connected for the touch sensor. And then I pass a pointer to the function that contains the code that I want to use for reacting to the touch event. And then the threshold, which is the value of the touch reading that will activate this interrupt. In the previous project, we used this code here and we used the value 20 as a value at which the entity would turn on and I'm going to use the same value as the threshold for the sketch in this example that I'll put in the touch attach interrupt function.

5-020_Touch_sensor_with_LED

```
 *  1. ESP32 Datasheet: https://www.espressif.com/sites/default/files/documenta
 *  2. esp32-hal-touch.h: https://github.com/espressif/arduino-esp32/blob/maste
 *
 *  Created on March 27 2019 by Peter Dalmaris
 *
 */

const byte LED_GPIO = 32;  // Marked volatile so it can be read inside the ISR

void setup()
{
  pinMode(LED_GPIO, OUTPUT);
  Serial.begin(115200);
  delay(1000); // give me time to bring up serial monitor
  Serial.println("ESP32 Touch Test");
}

void loop()
{
  Serial.println(touchRead(T4));  // get value using T4

  if (touchRead(T4) < 20)         // The value 20 is determined experimentally
    digitalWrite(LED_GPIO, HIGH);
  else
    digitalWrite(LED_GPIO, LOW);

  delay(500);
}
```

All right. Now, let's have a look at the sketch and what it looks like with the touch interrupt used. If the first part looks the same. I have the LCD GPIO set to 32 and I define the threshold being 20, which I determined experimentally. And then I use a variable called touch for detected attach four because I'm using the touch for a pin, which is chip io 13. So just to make it easy for me to remember which touch pin I'm talking about, I name this variable touch for two, touch for detecting some variable that I use to communicate between the main loop and the service interrupts routine and I initialize it to force this function. Here. Go to touch is the interrupt service routine that I have declared inside the touch attach interrupt. So I leave this aside for a second and go into setup where all the usual bits and pieces of the set up happen in the beginning. And then in line 69 I call the touch attach interrupt in passing the appropriate parameters. So first is the pin that I want to use for the touch event.

```
54 int threshold = 20;  // This threshhold is determined experimentally. If the touch
55                      // sensor returns a value below this number, the interrupt is triggered.
56 bool touch4detected = false; // Use this variable to communicate between the loop and the interr
57                              // routine.
58
59 void gotTouch(){
60  touch4detected = true;
61 }
62
63 void setup()
64 {
65   pinMode(LED_GPIO, OUTPUT);
66   Serial.begin(115200);
67   delay(1000); // give me time to bring up serial monitor
68   Serial.println("ESP32 Touch Test with interrupt");
69   touchAttachInterrupt(T4, gotTouch, threshold); // Attach the interrupt pin T0 to the service r
70 }
71
72 void loop()
73 {
74   if (touch4detected)          // The value 20 is determined experimentally
75   {
76     digitalWrite(LED_GPIO, HIGH);
77     Serial.println("Touch detected");
78     touch4detected = false;
79     delay(500);
80     digitalWrite(LED_GPIO, LOW);
81   }
```

Then, of course, a pointer to the interrupt service routine, which is called Touch, can use any name you like here as long as it's the correct name for a function. And then the threshold is the number that I chose to use that will trigger this interrupt, which again experimentally decided that it should be 24. The kind of wire that I'm using and the tension I'm getting from it when I touch it. So I should actually make a correction. I just noticed here should be t for so when I touch the of wire and the value that is read by the touch interface is less than 20, then this function could be called. Now, inside this function, what I do is I take a touch for the detected variable and turn it to true and the interaction retains must be very very quick. Whatever they do should take the minimum amount of time. So this way in here I only do one thing and that is to store the value true inside this variable. Then we go into the loop and the loop continuously executes, which you can do whatever else you want to do in that loop. But in this example, the only thing I do is to check if the touch detected is true or false. And if it's false, I'm not going to get into the F block, which is going to return back to the beginning of the loop. But if touch for detected is true, then we'll go inside this block, turn the LCD on, print a message to the serial monitor, and then change the value of the touch for detected to false so that we don't get back into the same. If we look again, the next time we get back into this F block will be when actually the code touch routine is called and the touch for value becomes true again. I want to keep the LCD on for half a second and then I'll turn it off. That's exactly what happens here. Touch on for half a second and half again. Okay, So there you have it. This is how you can use it and use the touch sensors to detect a touch event. And in this case, we use the hardware efficiently because you're still introducing delays in the loop, which are blocking the rest of the program execution. We use interrupts.

PHOTORESISTOR

All right. In this project, I'll show you how to use a photoresistor to detect light or to measure the intensity of ambient light. So this would probably already be known. The fourth resistor is simply a resistor, the value of which changes depending on how much light hits its surface. It's an analog sensor, so it will be using one of the ESP 32 GPUs configured as an analog input. Having a look at the typical map on my diagram here, we learn that there's a bunch of GPI areas that are useful as inputs only that can be used as GPIO outputs, but in fact any of the available chip areas can be used as an input or an output. And I have connected the measuring pin of my photo register here to GPO 36. This one right here. It's just more convenient because of the way that the components are laid out on my foot.

But you could have used any of the other GPI years. Let's have a look at some more details about the way that I've connected the components. So it's oriented like this. So I've got the resistor here that has one pin connected to the 3.3 volts to this. Been here connected to 3.3 pin, fourth pin on the ESP three to and then I've got that in series with a ten kilo on resistor it's this resistor right here which goes to ground. The measuring pin comes from a junction between the for the resistor and the fixed resistor. And it goes to the sense of the end which she can see in my map. The end is actually pin 39.

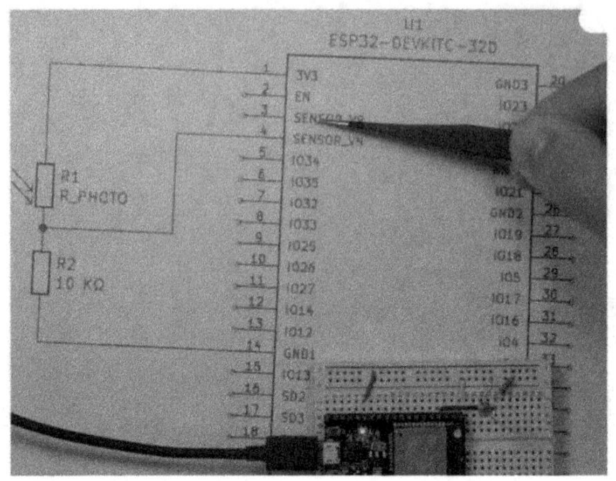

So this is a voltage ladder. And if you're not familiar with what a voltage ladder is, you can have a look at my other course. The basic electronics for making a make are quite a few projects specifically dedicated to the voltage ladder configuration. All right, let's have a look at how this sketch works before we go in-depth and have a look at it line by line. So here's a sketch. I'm just going to upload it and hold the IT button down in order to get my SB three two into uplink mode here again, I'll be okay and bring up the stereo monitor. This is the range coming out. So I've configured the four by default actually and I look at digital converters on the HP three to emit 12 bit numbers. So they have a 12 bit resolution which you can configure and I'm going to show you how you can configure that. So right now the value is around 3200. The range for a 12 bit number is up to 4010 95. She goes from here to 4095. So 3200 It means that the lights have security all for putting my hand over the sensor so you'll see the value dropping. I'll take my flashlights, my bike, flashlight, then shine the beam right on the sensor. You go so you can see that it maxes out the value. 4095. All right.

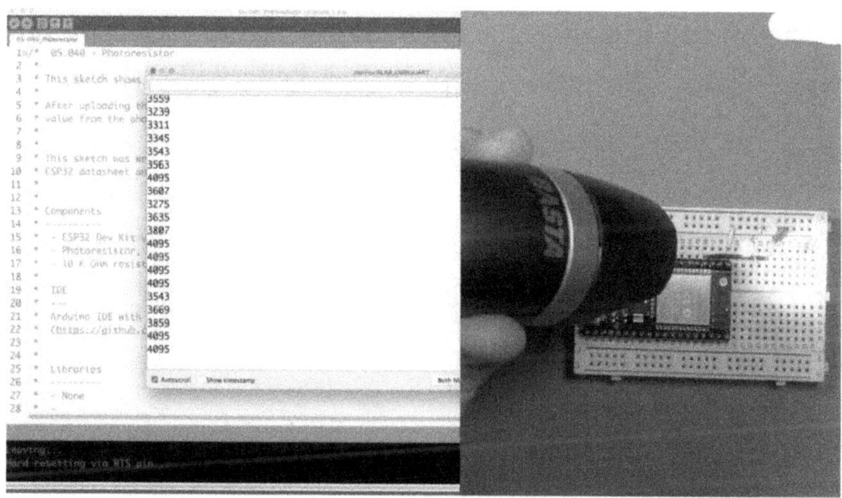

I can also use a proto since I'm only printing a single number on a monitor. So good the tools and bring up the serial plotter and I can see the same information, but no visually plotted here. So that is the intensity of the ambient light right now in my lab. Just cover the sensor with my hand. You can see that the value drops. If I take my flashlight again and place the beam right on the sensor, I can see the value rise. All right. Let's have a look at the code and how it works. You can have a look at the analog to digital converter code in the ESP 32. I do know for source code, this is this file here. Take a look at it and you see there is quite a lot of functionality available here. But the only one that we use is the analog read just called analog read Pass the pin that you want to read and it will give you back an integer in the default 12 bit resolution. If you want to change that resolution to something else, then you can use this function analog, read resolution and pass in here a number of bits from 9 to 12, and that's what I've done here. I've set the GPIO for the photo resistor to 39 bits measuring PIN, started the serial monitor and then simply called the analog read on this pin to send back a value the rec value.

```
typedef enum {
    ADC_0db,
    ADC_2_5db,
    ADC_6db,
    ADC_11db
} adc_attenuation_t;

/*
 * Get ADC value for pin
 * */
uint16_t analogRead(uint8_t pin);

/*
 * Set the resolution of analogRead return values. Default is 12 bits (range from 0 to 4096).
 * If between 9 and 12, it will equal the set hardware resolution, else value will be shifted.
 * Range is 1 - 16
 *
 * Note: compatibility with Arduino SAM
 */
void analogReadResolution(uint8_t bits);

/*
 * Sets the sample bits and read resolution
 * Default is 12bit (0 - 4095)
 * Range is 9 - 12
 * */
void analogSetWidth(uint8_t bits);

/*
 * Set number of cycles per sample
```

If I wanted to set the analog read function to a nine better solution or something else between nine and 12, then I would call the analog set width function. Change that to nine. Actually, let's do it. You'll see that a different range of numbers comes back. So uploading through a set, the board and bringing up the serial monitor. You can see that I've got a different set of numbers based on the chosen resolution of nine. Is it that Max is down to five? 11 is the maximum number. All right. So that's all there is to it. Of course, as I said earlier, having the delay here is not really an optimal way to use the hardware in the next couple of projects, especially in the project in the BME sense in which I show you how to use interrupt the time interrupts. To be more specific, we can set a one of a timers that come with the ESP 32 to trigger the call of the interrupt service routine and therefore get a new reading from the sensor instead of just putting a blocking delay of 500 milliseconds here half a second so that you can use that method that I'll show you in that upcoming project on the BME 282 essentially trigger any kind of functionality you want, you want in any kind of period. So just let me know about this. Now, the delay using delay in their dino sketch or the ESP 32 sketch of course is an easy way to go about it, but it's inefficient. So keep an eye in the upcoming project to learn how to avoid using delays and instead use timer interrupts. And just one last look here in the source code. I just want to point out there's a lot of other functionality you can use. Of course, it said that with the rush hour you had to do a minute ago, but you can also do things such as set cycles, set samples, clock divider and so on. I invite you to play around with these functionalities and see how and see how you can use them in your sketch to get samples from your analog sensors. Just a bit of experimentation to understand how these work. But in this case, such as yours, the simplest possible way to get everything from the photoresistor. Okay, now let's move on to the next project where I'll show you how to use the digital sensor Bmy 280 to take temperature and barometric pressure readings and also calculate the altitude based on those readings. And first, I'll show you how to do this in the simplest possible way, using delay in your loop. But then in the next project after that I can show you how to use timer interrupts with sync, which I think is a very interesting topic. So let's check it out.

BME280 ENVIRONMENT SENSOR USING I2C

Keeping time with the dedicated real time clock. These three, two, three, one. I'm going to show you in this project how to set it up and how to think of the time and date on it and read it out and print it on the serial monitor. And then in the following projects, I'm going to show you how to display this information from the real time clock on a nice quiet C LCD screen like this one here that we've learned about in previous projects and also how to use a very interesting feature of this module, which is the square wave generator. It's one of the pens here and the S cute W produces shockwave waves, a very accurate frequency that we can use, among other things, to create external interrupts and do things in our history. Three two without having to use delay function and have very precise timing. But we'll talk about that in a later project. First, let's have a look at the module itself. So the integrated circuit provides us with date to calendar and time capped capabilities and then how we can connect the module to our ESP through to the end via a library.

We had to use it in our sketches. Just have a look at the data sheet first. So this is a sheet for the D is 3 to 3 one. You can find your real location here in the sketch for this project and I have it in number four in my other information list and from this data sheet we learned that this is a very accurate RTC module that manages all sorts of timekeeping functions. So of course we can tell we can use it to tell the time and the date. It also has a very accurate thermometer. It can tell the temperature from -40 degrees Celsius to plus 85 degrees Celsius. As I mentioned earlier, it has a square wave output signal and it also has a pin that provides a very accurate 32 kilohertz signal from the on-board oscillator. And I'm going to show you what those look like on the scope later. And a lot more information here about the module that you can obviously have a detailed look at, if you wish, in terms of the library that we'll be using in this example.

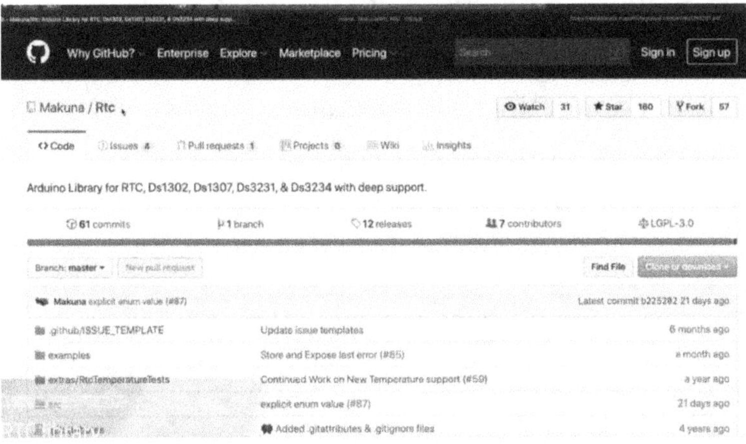

It's this one here by M Acuna. So the RTC Library, there's a lot of other libraries available as well that work both with the Arduino and with the ESP 32. But I thought that this one particular issue, very well written, performs really well and scored all the functions that we need to take advantage of the capabilities of this module. So we'll be using this in these examples. This also wiki with information on how to use the library and examples and other documentation, very well documented project and the euros for both the library and the wiki here in the sketch and other information before we upload the sketch on the spirit to and have a look at how it works, let's check out the wiring. I've got my schematic here. This is an ice squared C device, so we use SD A and C L connected to our GPO 22 and GPO 21. And then for Voltage, in this example, I'm taking 3.3 walls from the first pin of the ESP32 although this module can also work at five volts. So in the examples coming up where I'll be displaying the date and time information and an LCD screen, I'll be connecting this module to the five volts pin so that we can also drive the LCD screen.

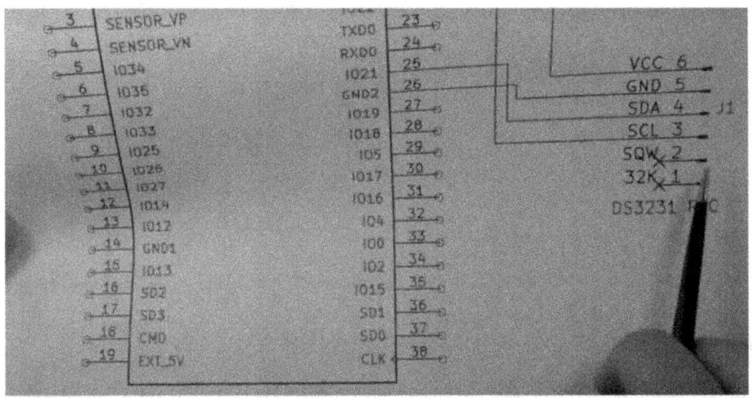

We said with a single wire instead of needing one power supply three walls for the clock module and another power supply at five watts for the LCD. So this is our fourth final polar in this world. And finally, don't forget the ground is connected to any of the ground panes of the ESP 32. For the time being, we're going to leave the q W and three to K pinch and connected. I'm going to show you what comes out of those pins in the third project in this section where we'll visualize the output on the oscilloscope. Okay, let's have a look at this sketch now.

And before I walk it through, I'd like to upload it and show you how it works and what the output is on the serial monitor. So compiling and uploading, holding down the boot button to enable the upload and. Okay, let's bring up the serial monitor. And every 10 seconds new readings from the date and the time should come out plus the temperature. So here it is. Now, what happens if I disconnect or remove the module actually from the bed port and notice that I've got a battery attached to the module. So the battery they have allows the real time clock to retain the date and time even when it's not connected to main power.

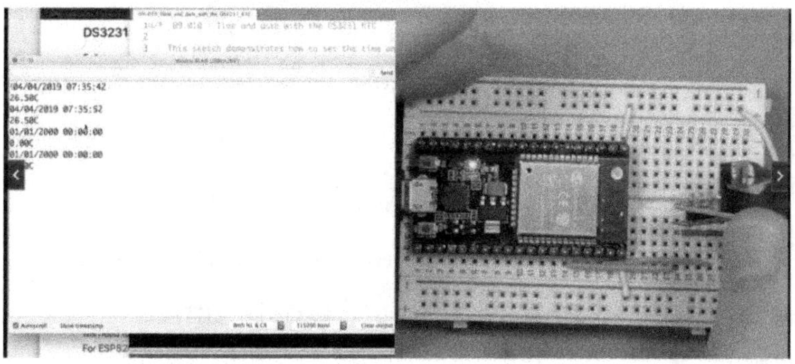

So I'm going to plug it back in and we can see that the date and the time is retained. However, if I remove the battery, you use my tweezers to try it out. So no battery, no power. The date and time information should be lost. Plug it back on the breadboard and there is the new date and time information. Obviously incorrect. So the date and time information has been lost. And let's have a look at the sketch to see how we can calibrate against it. It can go back to the current time and date. So before I do that, I'm going to put the battery pack on because I'd like a calendar and a time to be corrected. All times are right. So in this sketch, the first thing that happens is to call and include the wire library in the RTC. 3-3, two three, one. Just a quick look in the library repository and GitHub got into the CRC directory and you'll see that in here we've got multiple libraries and head of files because I'm using this three, two, three one real time clock. I'll be using this particular library. So that's why I'm including this here. So creating this header and then I create the RTC object inside the setup. Now let's go down a call to the begin function for the real time clock objects or start the object and communicate with a clock. And then here in line 75, what I do is I create a new RTC date time object. I call it compile and I initialize it with the RTC date time.

And then in the parentheses I've got underscore, underscore, date and underscore, underscore time. What happens is that during compilation these are compilation directives. So during compilation the compiler is going to inject the current date and time in here. And with the RTC date time constructor, this RTC DateTime object will be created which contains the current date and time, and I'm also printing it out here as well. Can you reset my especially to in a few seconds to show you the output that comes from line 76 and 77 and displaying the contents of the compiled variable, which is sort of type RTC date time. Why that is important is because here in line 80 and we use there is date time and a valid function to check if we have a correct date and time. And if we don't have a correct date in time and we go down to line one or two, we will use the set date time function to set the the clock to whatever date time information we have inside the compiled variable, which, as you know, is the date and time where this sketch was compiled last. So this sketch was compiled last a couple of minutes ago. So at this point, once we call this set date, the time function will have the date and time where that sketch was last compiled, inserted and stored in the real time clock. And then we can continue from there. So before we actually continue, I'm going to reset the ESP 32 and store the date and time where the sketch was last compiled onto the RTC.

All right, so could you stop with the scroll so you can see here date compiled which this and here is the date time object, which is the compiled object. It's 735 now. 741 So about 5 minutes ago I lost confidence and then the date and time was written in the RTC. So from this point onwards, my RTC module would contain the current date and time minus a few minutes. Because my compilation is a bit old, I might actually just recompile the whole thing again to get the accurate time on the module. Okay, so I recompiled the sketch, the date and time information stored on the real time clock was adjusted based on the compilation time and now the latest one is 742 and 15 seconds, which is that time that I see on my computer up here as well. Okay, so that's how the time is set on the clock. Continue with what's happening in the setup function. We check to see that the RTC module is running and if it is running, then we set it to true. Set is running. We know at this point that everything is good. Then we get the date and time just to see what the current date and time on the clock is. And then compare it with compiled. And this is how we can make an adjustment, even though the date and time is stored already on the real time clock. If it is falling behind for some reason compared to the date and time of the last compilation based on this statement, we just reset it. So this is a second condition by which the date and time is set on the clock. If it's running behind the compiled time and date. So with all these calibrations, we finally have the correct date and time stored in the RTC module. A couple of things to do at the end of the setup function is to turn off the 32 kilohertz pin and the front print produced into square wave pins. So these two pins here, we just turn both of those off. Going to show you how these two work in the next project. So we're going to be using these two pins now in the loop. We simply use the get date and time function store that is now variable, which is of type RTC date time, and then we'll call the print date time function in bit by bit format and print out the date and time in the serial monitor. So here's this function. It receives a pointer to the RTC date time function and will use the send print f underscore p function to format the string that we want to store inside the date string variable, which is just an array of cards and print it out to the serial monitor. And since print F is a C function that receives an array of characters, it needs to know how big that array is. And then we use a formatting string like this one here to create this new string and store it in the date string array of characters before we call the print function to print it out. If you want to know more about how all of this works, and especially if you want to know more about the and the scope p variation of the s and print F function, have a look at the documentation that I've linked to up here. It will hopefully make all of this much clearer, but this is just a common way of manipulating the format of a string and creating it on the fly and at the same time preserving RAM because we do all of this work in the flash memory. That's what the star does. So this is a macro that stores this string in flash memory so we can reuse it many times without having to take up any memory in RAM. Okay. So that's it. With this introductory project to the DS 3 to 0 one in the next project, I'll show you how you can print out the date and time information on an ice switch. Same LCD.

THE ESP32 DEV KIT

Let's have a look now at the ECB. Three, two. They've kicked off a development kit for its latest version. At the time I'm recording this in the image here, you can see the ESP three two and the development kit on which the ECB 32 module is situated. And what the ESP three to death kit does for us is to expose the ECB modules, and at least some of those to the outside world. So I'm highlighting the pins that come out of the ECB three two modules right here. And those are exposed to the pins that you see at the edges of the development kit so that we can plug our development kit on a breadboard or another piece of be and then make use of its resources.

When I updated this project in June of 2022, I tested the various experiments with the pictured ESP three to Death

Kit, which is also marked as the fourth vision for this kit contains the ECB three two Rule 32 EE Module, which I discussed in the previous project and is an update of the ESP 310 Rune three to the board pictured in this slide still fits nicely in a mini breadboard, and I've used it to test all of the experiments in this project. In my last market survey I found that this point is not as easy to find as the generic USP 32 deficit with a room 32 module, but you can find it at retailers like DG, K and Mouser. The main physical difference between the pictured official board and the generic board is that in the official version for board the antenna extends outside the main board along the top of the board and that the board has provision to be used with the slightly larger ESP three to Rover E module. Notice here that there are unused pads adjacent to pens 2526 18 and five that are taken up by the rover module. Apart from the updated SB 32 module, the generic and official dev kit boards that have tested worked practically the same. The core hardware that is present on the development kit, things such as the USP two serial programing interface, the power subsystem that allows us to provide power to the module, push buttons for reset and for setting it to the upload mode indicator aids and a few other things. So in this sketch here, I've marked with numbers these most important components on the HP 32 dev kit.

ESP32 DevKitC V4

Supports the ESP32-WROOM-32 module with:

1. A micro USB port to serial programming interface
   a. Also provides power
2. Pushbutton for reset ("EN")
3. Pushbutton to enable firmware download mode ("BOOT")
4. Power on LED
5. Two rows of headers that breakout the module pins
   a. Compatible with regular breadboards
6. A programmable LED (attached to GPIO2)

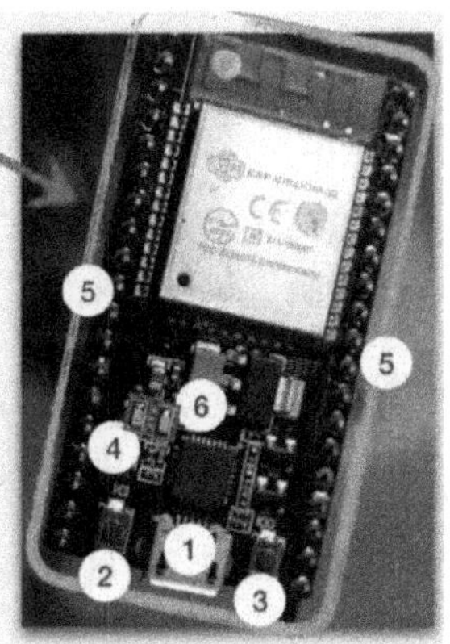

You can see number one is the USB-C connector, which is also the way that we provide power to the ESP module and uploader programs and also communicate with a serial monitor that is a micro USB port. I've got to push buttons marked number two and number three. So the number two push button is used for resetting a module and restarting the execution of a sketch that is already uploaded, while number three puts the module to upload mode. So they consented to a program from the Arduino idea. And you see me pressing on this button every time that I want to upload to a program from the TV. No idea. Then we've got a number for the power on LTE. So long as your ESP 32is powered that LTE will be on mark. This number six is another LCD, a Programmable LCD, which in the case of my development board is attached to GPIO to be worth it. Not all development kits have this programmable LCD. If yours doesn't have it, all you've got to do is just connect an external LCD to two pro two and you have the exact same functional team. Also missed an important aspect of this port, which are the two rows of headers marked five here. In this photo they break out the pins from the ESP 32 module so that they become compatible with the breadboard. And this is another really nice aspect of the SB 32 development kit as opposed to the ADRENO. It's the fact that the development kit is compatible with a pre put in. As you see, I hope to actually be using it almost exclusively plugged into my mini breadboard. A couple of other things that I haven't highlighted with numbers that I want to talk quickly about is this chip here. So this chip here is in charge of the USB communications and this one here is the voltage regulator. I've got another project coming up in this section in which I outline the power options that you have with the HP 32 module, which have to do with the three different ways by which you can power up your HP 32. Before we move on to the next project, I also wanted to mention that there's a variety of other development boards that host the USB three two module, such as the USB three, two, Lyra, the HP 32 PICO kit and a few others. I've got some of them showing in this slide. If you're curious about these boards, have a look at these, your rail down here where you can find more information about them. I shall show you what the ESP32 module looks like once we move the cover.

So let's do that right now. So removing the cover reveals the bear module and zoom in and we can now see the two integrated circuits in it. The larger one, this one here is the SB 30 2d0wdq6 microcontroller and this slightly smaller chip right here is the SPI flash memory. So now you know what is beneath the cover. Okay, let's move on to the next project where we'll do a comparison between the HP 32 and what we know.

A CLOCK WITH AN LCD AND THE DS3231

Hi. This project will take this circuit from the previous project a step further and include an ice squared c LCD to display the date and time information and, of course, a temperature as well. So I'm combining the sketches from the previous project, plus the sketch that you looked at in a previous section on displays where I showed you how to connect and I squared the LCD to your speaker to show the circuit. We've got two devices that share the same ice quite c bus in the circuit.

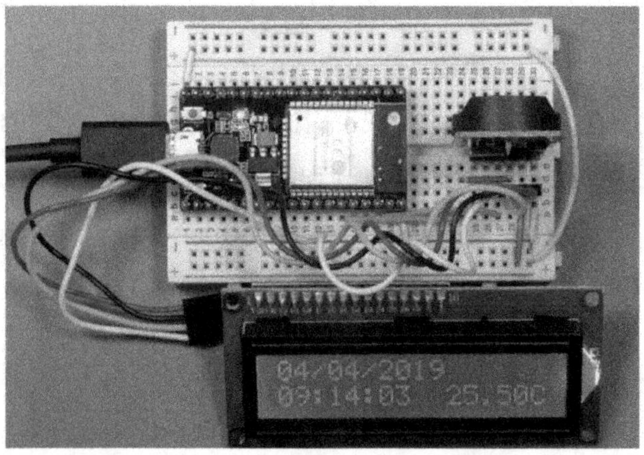

Have a quick look at it first before we go to the sketch showing the circuit. We've got this situation, this wiring. We've got two devices. The real time clock and the ice squared C LCD, and those share the FDA and C L lines that are going to GPIO 22 and GPIO 21 on the HP 32 Now because the ice quit C was the module requires five folds for it to operate. I've connected both the real time clock module and the LCD to the 5/4 line on the SB three two. And as I said in the previous project, the S 3 to 3 one module is perfectly happy working either at five volts or the 3.3 volts.

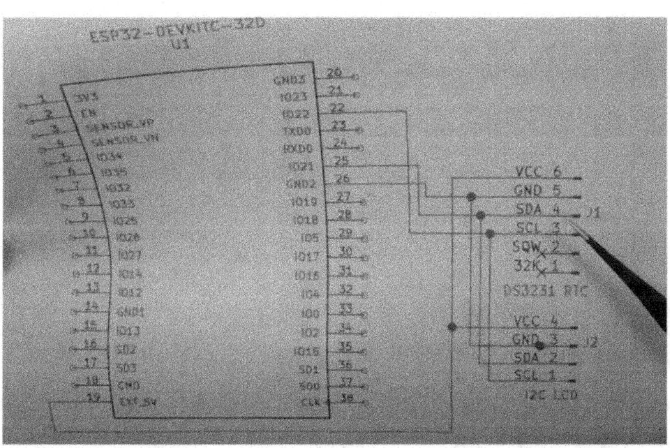

I could have connected them separately, so could have connected the real time clock to the 3.3 volts him and the ice qubit C module for the LCD two five votes on for just using a single five volt power rail here on the breadboard. Just simplify the schematic like that. Save one wire. So that's all there is to the wiring. I 'll look at the sketch now. I've already uploaded the sketch and it's operating. I'm still printing the values on the serial monitor, but we don't really need it anymore. Since we have the information we can on the LCD screen.

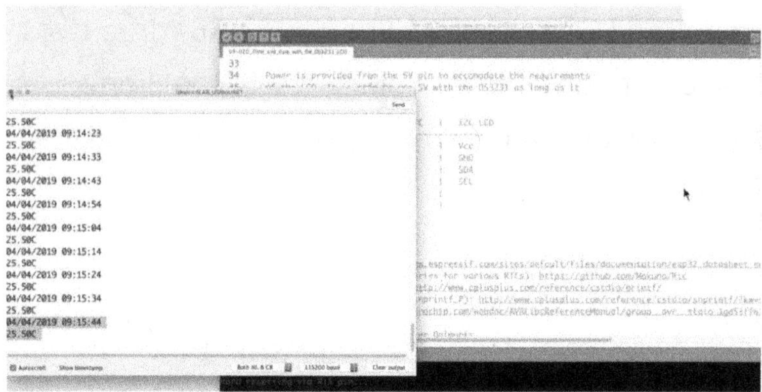

So for this sketch to operate, we need to have the two libraries so they see RTC CDs 32310 and we create the RTC object here in line 64. And then we also import the liquid crystal and school I squared c y to see how and create this object here the LCD object to control the screen and the tumultuous operation on different eyes could see addresses. So there is no conflict to worry about inside the setup. You already know what's happening in the second part of the set up all the way down here. And the only difference between the previous project in this project is that now I am also setting up the LCD object to initialize it and then turn on the backlight in the loop. Again, we get the current date and time and store that in the now variable. Then call the print date time function just like we did in the previous project. I preserve that down here exactly as we did in the previous project. On top of that, I'm also calling the update LCD function. That's a new function. I'm passing the now object with the current date and time, and I'm also passing the result of the quality get temperature function from the RTC object because I also want to print out the temperature on the LCD screen. So we now go to the update LCD function in it to create arrays of characters, one to hold the date string so one will print out the first line. I will eventually contain the first line. And the second one is for the time string. So the second one will print out or contain a text there piece here on the second line of the LCD screen and exactly as we did in the previous project where we show the print date time function here I'm using the as in print if on this copy function to create the string first for the first line, it contains a month, day and year and for the second line that contains the hours, minutes and seconds.

```
  lcd.print(datestring);
  lcd.setCursor(0, 1);
  lcd.print(timestring);
  lcd.setCursor(10, 1);
  lcd.print(temp.AsFloatDegC());
  lcd.print("C");
}

void printDateTime(const RtcDateTime& dt)
{
  char datestring[20];

  snprintf_P(datestring,
             countof(datestring),
             PSTR("%02u/%02u/%04u %02u:%02u:%02u"), // Construct the string in flash memory. Use prin
             dt.Month(),
             dt.Day(),
             dt.Year(),
             dt.Hour(),
             dt.Minute(),
             dt.Second() );

  Serial.print(datestring);
}
```

```
Leaving...
Hard resetting via RTS pin...
```

And I can remind you if you want to learn more about s in print f on this copy and the macro, have a look at the information here. Just have a look at those links. All right. And then at the end of this function, I also print out the temperature. So that's all there is. That's pretty straightforward as you can see, this example is fairly simple, but it's got one big disadvantage and that is the use of a delay function. So in line 153, I introduce a delay function to put in 10000 milliseconds so that the LCD screen is updated with a new time and date every 10 seconds. And while that is happening, the sketch is blocked here. There's nothing else other than just counting milliseconds.

WIFI CONNECTION

Hi. This is the first project in this section dedicated to the East B 32 Wi-Fi capability. And I'm simply going to show you how you can get your ESP32 connected to your local wifi network. Just before we get into that, just remind you that the wi-fi is one of the two main communications capabilities built into the ISP. Three two. The other one is Bluetooth. The Speaker two has the ability to use both the classic version of Bluetooth and also barely Bluetooth low energy. And I'm going to show you how to use those in our coming up section in a separate section. So let's begin with wi fi. In this project, I'm simply going to use the board itself with no external components.

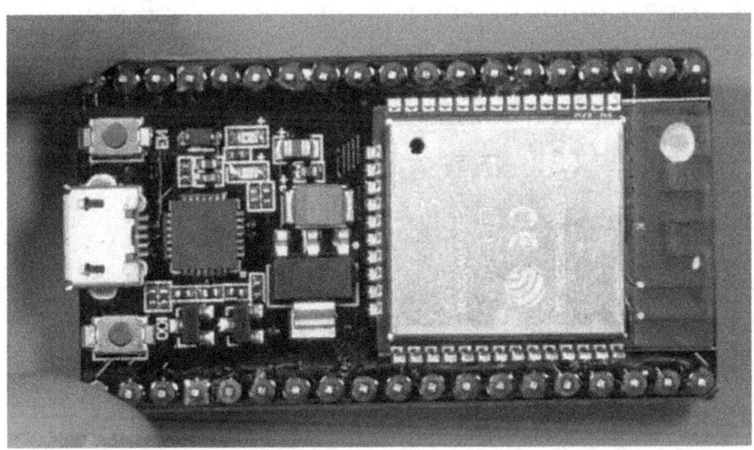

It's in a way, the Hello World Program for Wi-Fi Connectivity. And I'm going to show you the minimal code needed to connect your facility to the Wi-Fi network. It's not going to do anything other than connect to your network and just walk through the various functions that are needed and also have a look at the source code. So let's have a look at the example sketch. Here. It is a modified version of one of the examples when you install the do not use P3 to core capability to your I do know IEEE, you get a bunch of examples with it. So if you go to file examples, go ahead down here where it says wi fi and there's a bunch of examples here that you can look at. And once you are familiar with wi fi at the end of this section, I really think it's a good idea to go and have a look at these and see what else is possible, because I'm not going to be covering all of those. For example, one that I think you will be very interested in is this one here, the Wi-Fi access point, which converts your ISP 3 to 2. What the name of this example says is an access point so that other devices can connect to it. So check it out in later projects in this section. And once again to show you how you can use wi fi client secure library to add encryption and security to your network. Another thing that you should have a look at is the source code for the various libraries that will be using.

10-010_WiFi_connection

```
/*  10.010 - Connection to a Wifi network

   This sketch simply connects the ESP32 to a Wifi network.

   Once the connection is made, nothing else happens.

   This sketch was written by Peter Dalmaris using information from the
   ESP32 datasheet and examples.


   Components
   ----------
    - ESP32 Dev Kit v4

    IDE
    ---
    Arduino IDE with ESP32 Arduino Code
    (https://github.com/espressif/arduino-esp32)


    Libraries
    ---------
    - WiFi (comes with the ESP32 Arduino core)
```

So I've got links to the source code for the specific libraries that we'll be using in the sketch as usual in the sketch itself. But at this point I just draw your attention to the wifi folder here. This folder contains the source code and various examples, and in the source code you've got the classes specifically related to wi-fi. We're not going to be using all of those classes. Some of those are going to be used. The class contains the functions that we need for all of our examples here. Eddie Hedge Door Page. I guess this comes from the Internet and the Wi-Fi library and specific classes are built on the capabilities that the original Ethernet library from the original provided. So here for example, you find functions such as BEGIN, which is a function that we call here in the set up method. They go right here, we call wi-fi to begin, we pass the name of our network and a password to our network and basically this is what we call here.

```
10-010_Wifi_connection

const char* ssid     = "ardwifi";     // change this for your own network
const char* password = "ardwifi987";  // change this for your own network

void setup()
{
  Serial.begin(115200);
  delay(10);

  // We start by connecting to a WiFi network

  Serial.println();
  Serial.println();
  Serial.print("Connecting to ");
  Serial.println(ssid);

  WiFi.begin(ssid, password);

  while (WiFi.status() != WL_CONNECTED) {
    delay(500);
    Serial.print(".");
  }

  Serial.println("");
```

And if the connection is successful and the ease with Rita does connect to the Wi-Fi network, then it will return true Boolean and so on. But we'll see later. We also call functions such as local IP, which returns an IP address, which is what we do here. And so this is where the most important, the main functions for the Wi-Fi library are. All right, let's move on. Here's a sketch, very simple. We include the wi fi library. First we see why fight or hate speech files. Just have a quick look at that. Actually, this point before we continue just to show you what's in it. So if you go into why I would hate to show you is that it in turn includes all of these other libraries which contain the functions that we need. So it's a whole collection of files and classes here and next in two lines would create two constants. I wrote character arrays in which we specify the name of the network that we want to connect to and the password. And then we get into this set up function. We start a serial monitor. If we start the serial interface, I should print out a few messages. And this is where the connection actually happens. It's just a single line.

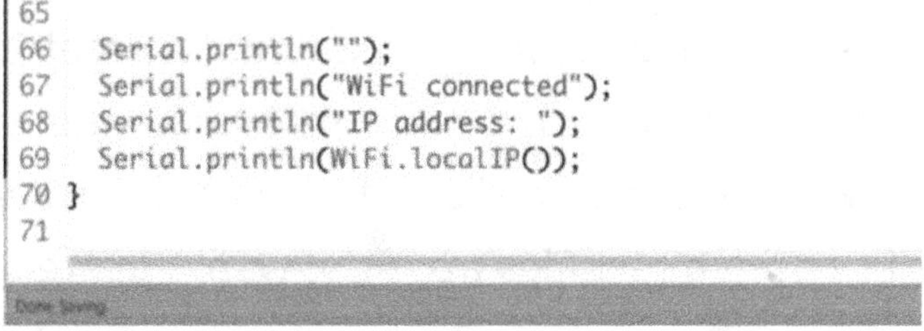

```
  WiFi.begin(ssid, password);

  while (WiFi.status() != WL_CONNECTED) {
    delay(500);
    Serial.print(".");
  }

  Serial.println("");
  Serial.println("WiFi connected");
  Serial.println("IP address: ");
  Serial.println(WiFi.localIP());
}
```

We find that we can we pass the name of the network and the password, the connection happens here. This will return either a true or false. So we could actually use this response, the return value from begin to check whether we're connected or not. But also we can call this status function and do the same thing at any point in our program. And that's what we do here. So while the Wi-Fi status is not connected, then we actually get stuck here. We stop. But if the Wi-Fi status is equal to connected, so this is the status returned when the wife when the HP 32 is connected to Wi-Fi. If this is true, then we'll just continue the rest of our program, print out the IP address so that we can continue with whatever else would do in this example. We're not actually doing anything at all inside the loop. So this is a totally useless example, which is, as I said, a hello world program for wi fi. But in the very next project, I'll show you how you can build on to this sketch and create a HTTP client which will go out, pick up a text file from somewhere on the World Wide Web and print its contents on the serial monitor. Later in this section, we are going to look at additional examples that provide us with more realistic applications for the wi fi module. We have a secure client, for example, which will use HTTPs to fetch text files from the web. We are also going to be learning how to send sensor readings to an Internet of Things service again, using our secure protocol. And we are also going to implement a web server. So let's plug it in, upload this sketch to my ESP 32 and make sure that it works. There's not much weight on the security, so I'm going to wait down with something it stable. Actually, we like that. That's okay. All right. Upload the sketch, hold down the boot button to get into boot mode. All right. And uploading now and start the serial monitor. Check my speed of communication. 115 200 looks. Okay, so I'm just going to rebooted. All right, There you go. So after my reboot, the wifi on the ESP 32 was connected to my test network and this is the IP address that it has been assigned by my test router. And also I should see this point before we move on to the next project. You see that? I've got details, information about the functions that are running on the HP 32. So these are additional logs that are coming out of it in addition to the printout from the sketch itself. And I advise you to also get those additional log messages printed out. And to do that, go to tools and then go to core debug level and just say debug. Otherwise you can go for none in order to keep the content of the ceremony to two to minimum. At this point, I want to know what is happening with the various events. For example, here you can see that the wifi is ready. When I rebooted the HP 42 and it went to start Stay connected, which means that at this point the ESP 32 can go connected to my test network and it got an IP address from the router. And here's the IP address and etc. in my information, the various network information. All right. So it was quite useless, but at least now we know that our air space 32 can connect to the global network. Let's move on to the next project where I'll show you how to convert your exquisite O2 into a very simple HTTP client.

WIFI HTTP CLIENT

Hi. In this project, we are going to build on what we've learned in the previous project. And once we have the ability to connect it to the local Wi-Fi network, we'll get it to go out into the web and fetch the contents of a text file which is stored on a web server. In my case, I've got the file that I'll keep getting the data out of on an Amazon S3 bucket, but it doesn't need to be that. It can be a text file. It's said to be stored on any accessible web server. Before we get into the details, I just want to show you this sketch working. I've already uploaded it to my ESP 32 and I'm going to start up the serial monitor and wait a few seconds for the authorities to go out and fetch that text. And here it is. When you stop all this crawl. So down here you'll see a line. Hello. This takes this stored in a remote file. And this is the content that I've actually stored inside this little test.

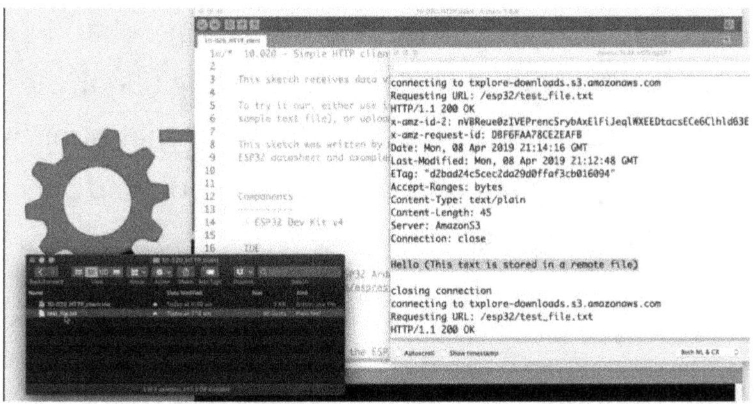

And this file was thought to actually have a look inside its contents. You'll see that it's hard. This text is stored in a remote file of the same thing that you see here in the serial monitor. This file is stored as set on Amazon S3. I've got a bucket here and inside that package. So here's the name of the packet. Inside that packet I've got a directory and inside this directory I've got a couple of text files. This is a file that my sketch just fetched. And this one here is another text file that I'll be showing you how it works in another project. It contains some information that controls and l'étape. I will talk about that. As I said in another project, let's make a little change just to be absolutely sure that this sketch works. And I want to make a little change to the information ID so the text file so that next time that this file is fetched, that change is also shown. So I'm going to open that with a text editor or any text editor will do, you know, just say here, hello again, exclamation mark. All right, now just save that. I'm going to upload this file to replace the existing file on Amazon with three strikes a drop Next, make that publicly readable. And next again, upload sort of one upload or one operation in progress.

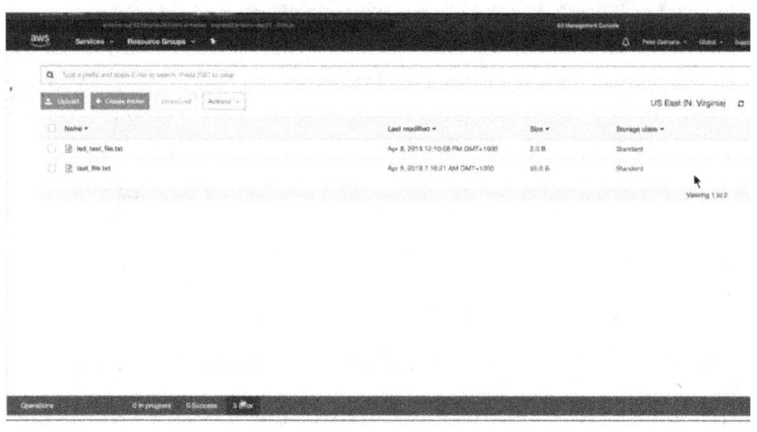

I'm not sure what the error is, but I can see here that the timestamp is correct. So the file has been uploaded and it's C, I'm going to go back to auto scroll and we've got hello again. So Inspector two was able to fetch the latest version of this text file. Another thing that I want to show you here is what happens in the serial monitor. Here is the HTTP response to the GET request that my ESP 32is sending out to the web server. So here you can see a couple of lines that tell me what is happening on those lines generated by the sketch itself. So we're going to come back to all this in a minute, but I just want to show you the interesting bits. So here is requesting your rail and then the URLs, just nothing fancy here, just normal serial print outs.

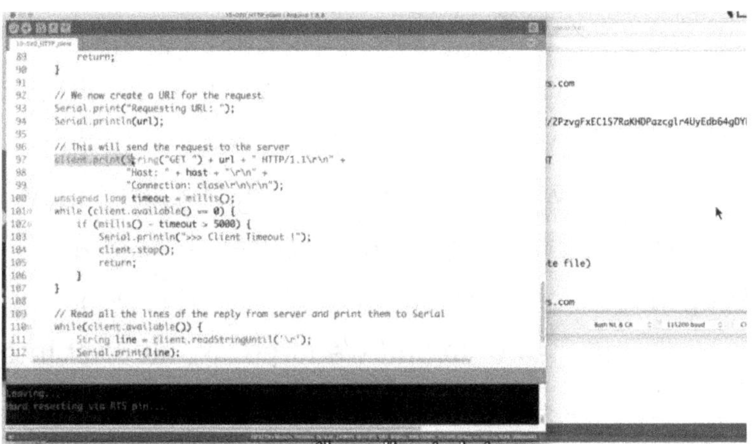

So I am requesting a tutorial. And then below that we've got the client dot print function to which we pass and actually construct on the fly the text string that represents the get request. So we use the plus function to stick strings together. So text that strings together. First we've got the HTP that gets followed by a white space or a single space. Then we have the URL. The URL is this string here and then we'll connect that or we append that to a blank space, followed by the version of the HTTP protocol that we're using, plus a return. So that will then generate the request in the header of our request. We also provide the host parameter. The host is the domain name for the web server. In this case, it's this thing here that I've got highlighted. It's a bucket on Amazon. It's three and then we'd simply close the connection and we wait for a response. So all that is happening on the SB 32 and then a few milliseconds later the web server responds with this. So this is the setup here in response to our get request. It contains two parts. The first part is the header, which I've highlighted here, and the second part is the payload which I've highlighted here, and they are separated by a blank line and of course the server sometimes may be busy doing other things. It may not be working at all, maybe down and we need to take that into account. And that's what happens here. So between lines 100 and 106, we've got a bit of code that counts the amount of time that it takes for the web server to respond. And if it takes over 5000 milliseconds or 5 seconds, then we just stop the client object in return. So we're still waiting at this point.

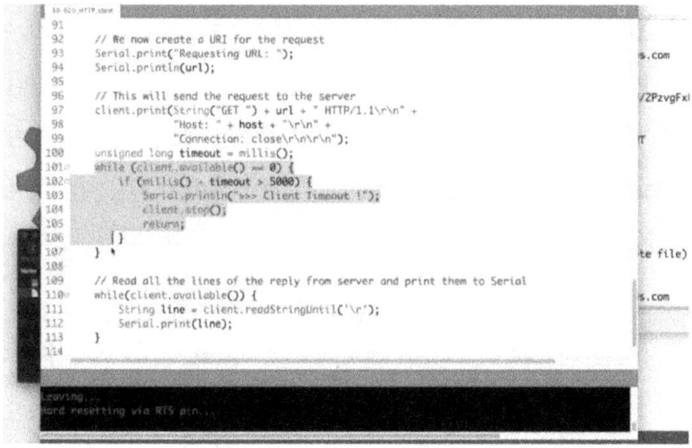

```
// We now create a URI for the request
Serial.print("Requesting URL: ");
Serial.println(url);

// This will send the request to the server
client.print(String("GET ") + url + " HTTP/1.1\r\n" +
             "Host: " + host + "\r\n" +
             "Connection: close\r\n\r\n");
unsigned long timeout = millis();
while (client.available() == 0) {
    if (millis() - timeout > 5000) {
        Serial.println(">>> Client Timeout !");
        client.stop();
        return;
    }
}

// Read all the lines of the reply from server and print them to Serial
while(client.available()) {
    String line = client.readStringUntil('\r');
    Serial.print(line);
}
```

```
Leaving...
Hard resetting via RTS pin...
```

But if the time is not out, it doesn't time out. Then the server responds within 5 seconds. Then we move on to this part of the code where for as long as the client has got the still available text in its buffers, so for as long as the client is still sending us text, we take the text one line at a time and then we print it out to the serial monitor. So this piece of code here is what emits all of this, because all of this is a response to how I get a request from this server that they submitted. That's how this sketch works. The bits that I made earlier are bits that you already know about. So here's where we include the Wi-Fi header so we can access the functions that come with wi fi. This is where we note down and we write the credentials for the Wi-Fi network. These two variables are new. So this is the host for the web server. In my case, it's my S3 bucket Plus. And these are real for the resource that we want to access. And then these two are combined later on in the loop to create the get request. And inside this setup we do the usual that are required in order to connect to the local Wi-Fi networks. All this is exactly the same as what you've learned about in the previous project. As you can see, it's fairly easy to create and see the client on your ISP. 32. The main problem here is that this client is not secured as you can see here, we'll create a client object from the Wi-Fi client class. We specify the to port to be 80, and then we use this information with our client dot connect function to create a connection to the remote web server. But this connection is not encrypted. It's the get request that goes out in the clear. You know, that is not a problem. For a little example. Like there's just no important information that is circulating around the Internet. But imagine other applications where security and encryption are important. Like you could be working on a security system, for example, or you may be transmitting sensitive data from your lab and things of that sort. Then you will want to be using DNS encryption and doing all your communication via the HTTPS protocol instead of being clear to the people. So I'm going to show you how to do exactly that in the next project where we'll use the same sketch as a framework and build on it the infrastructure needed for secure encrypted communications. So let's check this out next.

WIFI HTTPS CLIENT

Hi. In this project, we are going to work on the sketch from the previous project and then show that it's communication with the remote, whichever is secure. And it's happening over tennis and hedge tips. Therefore, this communication is encrypted. I have already uploaded this sketch to my SB 52, and let's have a look at this serial monitor to see it working. And they are connected. The server head is received. I'm afraid to hit it anymore because I'm not doing anything with him anyway and I'm simply printing out the payload. So the content of the text file is not obvious here, but this communication is actually going over page trips and all the text that you see travels through the internet encrypted, and then once it reaches the ESP 32, it becomes decrypted. So I'm going to show you how this works in the sketch. And the sketch is almost identical to what you saw in the previous project. Obviously, I've got a couple of things here that are important, such as these two certificates. I'm going to explain how you can generate those where you can get them from in a minute, but have a look at the setup function. The and function is identical to what you've seen in the previous projects. All it's doing is to get your ISP through, to connect it to the local wi-fi network and then inside the loop. The biggest difference is that instead of using the wi fi client, we now use the wi fi client secure class, which I think I've got here a wi fi client secure. So there's more information in here and details about how it works, but I'm going to give you a summary in this project anyway. So we have replaced wi fi client with wi fi client secure.

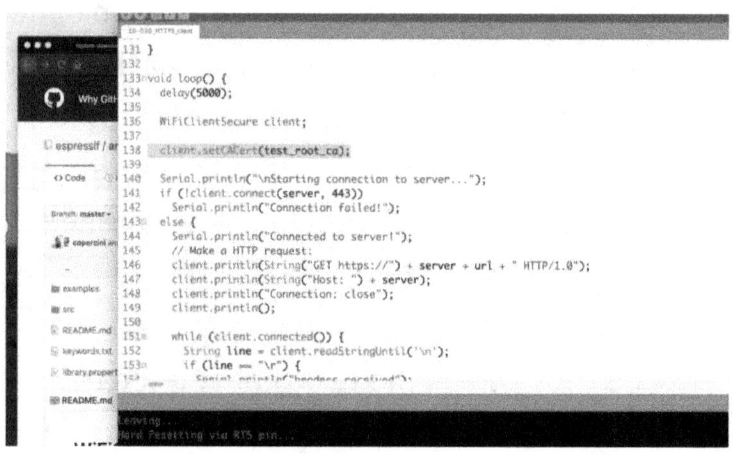

And another difference here is that we make a call to set a certificate and set the certification authority certificate. This certificate is a certificate that a web server uses in order to encrypt its communication with the web client. So we need to pass this certificate to this function into the client so that it can become part of this encryption and decryption process. Apart from that, everything else is the same. So once we've got the client configured with the specific service route, public certificate, then as you can see, the rest is the same. We're still using the connect function This time will connect to Port four, four three, which is where the protocol points to instead of port 80. And we'll just create the get request exactly what we did in the previous project and then listen for a client to connect and to send us its content. So let's talk a little bit more about this, about the Route certification Authority certificate. The certificate that you need to pass here depends on the server that you want to connect to. I've got a couple of examples here. I've got here the certificate for my own server and take expirations dot com. And now I also have a certificate for the Amazon S3 bucket way. The test text file is stored. The process of getting those certificates is exactly the same. So let's work with the S3 route certificate so that we can get with the so we can read the contents of this file here. And notice I used Firefox.

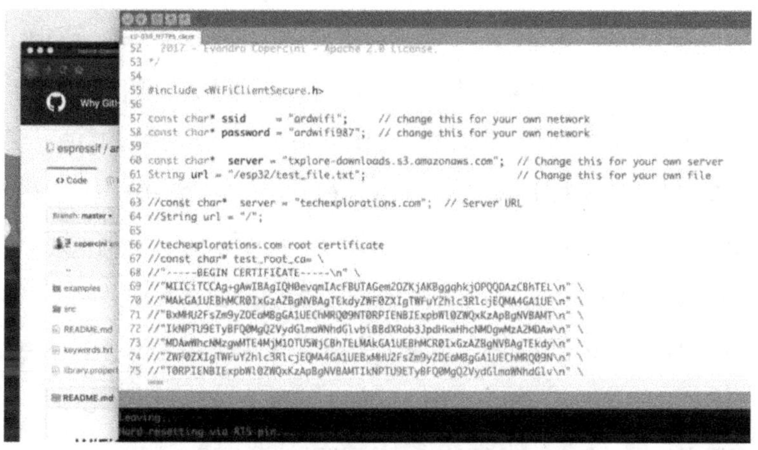

This is important. Firefox has a function that allows us to export and save locally a public route certificate for anything that is publicly accessible for any web resource or web server. This is publicly accessible. This may be possible to do through a Chrome plugin or a safari plugin or other browsers, but I'm not familiar with them. So for this particular example, I am using Firefox here in this type of browser to point my browser to the text file that my ESP 32is also accessing. So there is the server and the main name right here. And then I've got the year real for the resource, which is a text file after the first forward slash right here. And for the protocol, be sure to specify how the DPS look with the s here. But once you do that of course you will see this little text message, the contents of the text file, but you also see the green padlock. So let's start the process of extracting the root certificate from this Amazon three packet and saving it on the local computer. So first click on the Green padlock. Okay. You get the information and information that the connection secured. So click on the little symbol here to show the connection details. Okay. Get the certification authority here DG cert I and see and go for more information. So this window pops up more information about all this. Let's click on the view certificate because that's what we want to do. We actually want to see the certificate and finally, we want to go through the certificate details, not just the general information. There's the details now.

There's different levels of this certificate. There's a set certificate hierarchy.

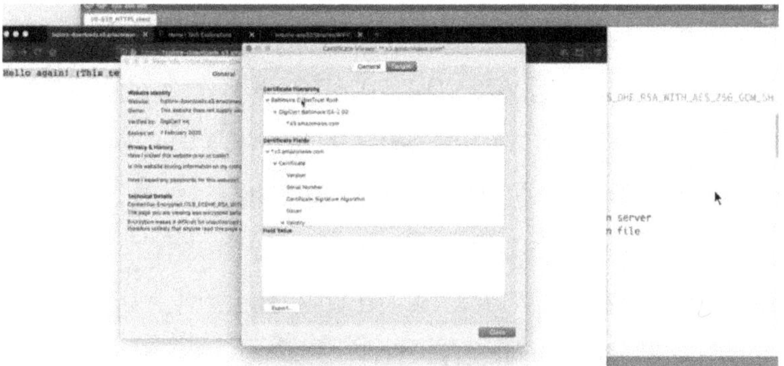

But what we want is the root certificate. So we want to click on Baltimore CyberTrust Root, this one here and now we have selected that root certificate. We want to export it and I'm going to save it in the downloads folder right there. Now we can close all that. We don't need it anymore. Here you'll see a new file, Baltimore Save that trust route. So this is the certification authority. Don't see our. Take a look at the contents of this file. I'm going to use text editing and download and open up this file and the contents. So this is the root certificate for the server that I want to connect to securely. And what I've got to do next is to copy this string into my sketch. Okay, before I show you how to use the certificate that you just got from

Firefox and jump in, it's now June 2022 and reviewing this project I realize that the Firefox method of getting the certificate seems to no longer be working and I was able to find an alternative to use. So I wanted to both keep the original just in case it might work with a future release of Firefox. And also that gives you an alternative to get the certificate. So this alternative has to do with using the open source libraries and the command line to extract the certificate. Just wanted to point out here that for example, here I'm using Firefox. In this case, the version of Firefox that I'm using is 101 .0.1. It was said in June 2022 and if I tried to do the same process or follow the same process that I showed you, just a couple of minutes ago in this video, you'll see that it doesn't work anymore. So here is the security window.

Certificate

*.s3.amazonaws.com — Amazon — Amazon Root CA 1

Subject Name

Common Name *.s3.amazonaws.com

Issuer Name

Country US
Organization Amazon
Organizational Unit Server CA 1B
Common Name Amazon

Validity

Not Before Wed, 15 Dec 2021 00:00:00 GMT
Not After Sat, 03 Dec 2022 23:59:59 GMT

Subject Alt Names

DNS Name *.s3.amazonaws.com
DNS Name s3.amazonaws.com

Public Key Info

Algorithm RSA
Key Size 2048
Exponent 65537
Modulus B5:5F:34:4C:D7:3A:1C:1D:DB:19:9F:82:31:29:C8:6B:AC:0D:7F:76:38:11:58 ...

Miscellaneous

If we have a look inside the certificate page, it looks like this and there's a bunch of certificates you can actually download. So for example, VPN as such, it's an individual certificate in the chain of certificates. It's also the image on tap here, which allows you to also download those two files plus the Amazon root certificate authority to file.

Okay. And none of those actually work for our purposes. So this method at this point in time, at least with Firefox, does not work. There may be other browsers that can give you this certificate, which I'm not aware of. Nevertheless, the SSL method always works. So here I am on my command line and I'm just going to issue this command here. It's an open SSL command, works a client and it says Just go to this location and grab to this URL and grab the certificate and other bits of information that are relevant and present them on the command line. So give it a few seconds to complete and the command is complete. Now I'm going to browse back and you'll see that there is a certificate chain. That's the first certificate with index zero, second certificate with index one and the third certificate with index two. And this is the certificate that we actually meet. So what you can do at this point is to copy this text and paste it in the sketch. Just as I'm about to show you in the next few seconds. So about a minute in this project, once you go through that, you'll be able to run the sketch, upload it to your ISP, and set it to. And as you can see here, I've already done that and it's working now. Let me continue with the rest of this project. I have already done that, of course, but it's going to show you really quickly got to be a little careful here because obviously it's a very long line to just do it in a single line. And the way that the certificates download it is called returns. At the end of each line, he had to be careful not to make any changes to it.

So the way that I do it is to first copy it. So copy and then paste it in my sketch and then just there carefully, very carefully, construct the string. And these backslashes at the end indicate that the string continues in the next line. So then start with the quotes. Each line must have a start and end quote. And then at the end you need to copy the backslash end, which is a carriage return that needs to be preserved in the string like that. But I've got one up here again, you only have to do this once, but oops, but you do have to do this one for each website or web resource that you want to connect to. Which meeting you here and and with a cynical like that. So now this is the certificate that I'll be using to configure the client so that this client and the remote work server can have encrypted communication. So of course I'm not going to use this because I already have it defined here, but that's all there is to do. So at this point, you know how to create a secure web client and you can use this web client to fetch data stored on a remote server. So the direction of communication is really from the remote server to your ISP. 32 We haven't really done anything interesting with this capability other than to just print the contents of the remote text file to the serial monitor. In the next project, we're going to show you how to use the same process so the same or the same sketch in order to control one of the episodes on the HP 32. So that way it can actually control hardware on your ISP to bypass information stored on a remote web server at a remote location. Let's check it out.

WIFI HTTPS CLIENT LED CONTROL

Hi. Now that you know how to create secure connections between your ESP 32 and which is on the Internet. Let's start thinking about some more useful applications. The first one that I want to show you is how you can use this functionality to control the chip areas of your ISP. 32. Just to keep things simple, I'm still not attaching any external hardware and I'm going to do a little demonstration of how you control the built-in LCD on the board, which is connected to GPIO. Number two. And in the exact same way you'll be able to control any other GPIO on your HP 32. So a little demonstration. What I've got here is a sample text file called edX. And this test and this call file thought to extend the text file contains a single byte. In this case, it's number one, but it could be number zero. Or it could be some other number. And I've uploaded this file to my S3 bucket on Amazon a w. S, and it's this one right here. The ECB 32 downloads this file every few seconds and checks the payload.

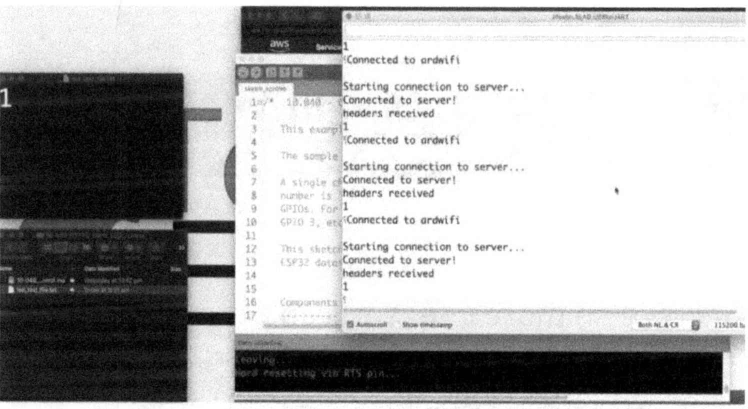

And depending on the value of the payload, which is the scroll, depending on the value of this payload, whether it's a one or a zero, it turns the ability on or off. If I change the content of this text file to zero, then save it and upload the new version to Amazon. Just click on the upload button and just wait for the new value to be fetched and the entity goes off very simple. I'm treating this payload as an integer and that allows me to have from zero all the way up to nine integers.

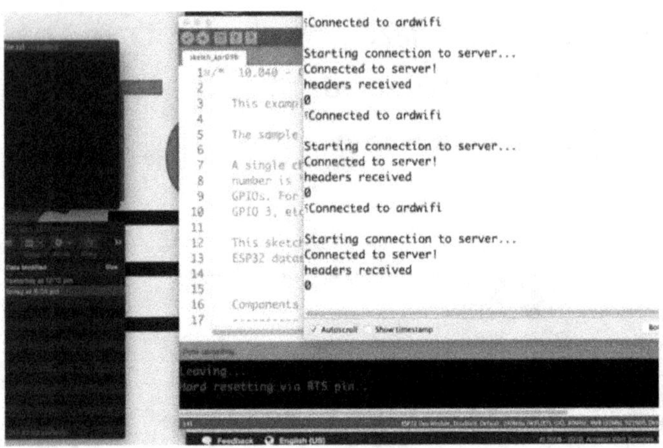

And depending on those integers I can get my ESP 32 to do different things like turn on and off, different GPIO, for example, not just a single POW. Alternatively, you can treat this number or this value here as a byte, in which case you get up to 255 values to play with, which you can basically use to control all of the bios, at least on or off and so on. But this is the simplest possible example to show you how you can control your HP 32 using a web resource. So let's have a look at how the sketch works and especially how the passage works, which is very simple, that you see nothing different to enlarge this a bit. So we can get as much of the sketch as possible on the screen. So nothing new here. You are familiar with all this from the previous project, including what's in set up. Let's go inside, loop in loop. Everything is the same. The new content that I have added is this right here. So after we have finished looking at the headers and we have received the headers, we go into the payload and look for the payload which just looks for the first byte. So client a variable will be yes, if there is there, if there's more bytes coming from the server and with car C equals client or read, we take a single byte from the buffer of the client stored inside C And then here we test to see what is stored in viable C and if it's a number one and will take the GPO in a bit too, too high.

And if it's a zero, we'll take it too low. And here you could test for other things. So for example, you could say if this was say a two, then you could go to GPIO three and turn it off or something like that. So you've got plenty of scope here to expand this loose sketch, but then you could be testing for bytes. Of course, that gives you a lot more flexibility. And then past all this, you could go for other ways of organizing information here so you could be looking for, say, the first in the second and the third character. So you could be passing here three characters or three bytes, and then you can have your client Uris b32 to first check to see what is in the first character and then check for the second character and do something else depending on the state of the second character. And then search for the third character and do something else. So you just keep track of how many characters you've read with just a little counter. So let's say just give you a quick demonstration, make an integer byte counter, start at the zero and then every time that a new character is read, you increment five counter by one and then inside your test, if it's a one or a zero, could go for plus byte counter like this. This is very rudimentary and very coarse. But what would happen here is that the first character in this example would control GPIO two. Now the second character controls GPIO number two plus one. So there will be two actually to correct this, I should put this down at the bottom. But so instead of looking at this again and hoping I'm not confused here the first time that this runs and we have the first character in sight, see? So that is correct. The number one got the first character inside the same then that would manipulate our IT typical plot and byte counter any DeSipio is to which we configured it up here in the byte variable constant and then the current value stored inside byte county zero. So that will give us an LCD connected to GPIO two. Now the second time that this runs, because we've got an increment on the byte counter, this would be two plus one and therefore would be manipulating any day connected to GPO three or a relay or something else.

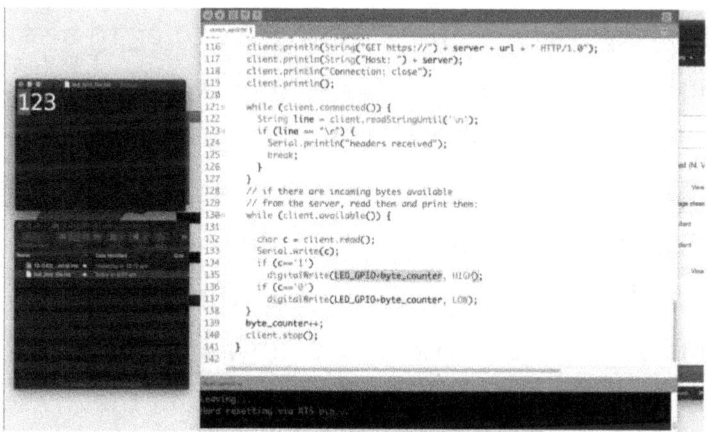

So let's say put in a valid value. The second entity which is connected to GPIO three would be turned off and then the white counter would increment again by one. And then the next time that this run would be manipulating to carry a to plus a new value for the byte counter, which is two. So there would be GPIO four and would turn it on and you can do things like that here in order to control the various CPUs or instigate other functionalities in your ECP three depending on the payload that your USB three fetches from the web.

INTRO TO CLASSIC BLUETOOTH

Hi. This is the first project of the section about Bluetooth. And in this project I'm going to do an introduction to Bluetooth classic. In the next project, I'm going to give you an example of a simple application that involves Bluetooth classic. And these LCD screens with the eyes qu'est CE backpack, and after that there's going to be a few projects on L e Bluetooth low energy, which I find very, very interesting because of the types of applications that you can create based on that technology. So first of all, actually, before we get into the hardware in the demonstration, I should explain what is the difference between the early Bluetooth, low energy and Bluetooth classic. So to do that, let's have a quick look at the Bluetooth article or Wikipedia tablet. It goes back a while. At the moment we are at least that vision for the Bluetooth protocol. So if you've purchased a Bluetooth gadget in the last three or four years, then most likely it will be running Bluetooth four. And you have a quick look at the Bluetooth form and the section here. And we learn that Bluetooth four includes two versions, one of them actually three versions, I should say, a classic Bluetooth that we're going to talk about and give a demo right now. And then there's Bluetooth, high speed and Bluetooth, low energy or barely Bluetooth high speed is based on Wi-Fi and the ISP, too. It's not equipped to use it, But the ISP 42 is equipped to use both Bluetooth classic and Bluetooth low energy with Bluetooth classic. What you can do is you can create applications that require a wireless serial connection between two devices that is sustainable.

So think of, for example, when you want to connect your wireless headset, for example, with your phone so they can have all your conversations without having to hold the phone on to your ear. This is a Bluetooth classic application, but on the other hand, think of something like this. This is a heart rate monitor. It doesn't require constant connection with a client like a device. It will read the information that the monitor is sending it, then display the heart rate at any given moment. But it only needs to send short bursts of data. So every second or every 10 seconds from this device here, which is the Bluetooth low energy server to a device that will read that data later on, I'm going to show you an application where we use the ESP 32 as a client to this device here and display that value. And not only that, but this device here only has a very small battery. And we want it to last for a long time. So we want this device to consume very little energy, hence Bluetooth, low energy. So this would be highly likely to use classic Bluetooth. Another thing that you can consider is this keyboard. I've got a keyboard here. This needs to be constantly connected to my computer since I'm constantly typing. And this is an example of an application of Bluetooth classic always on connection. So I hope this explains the difference. And you can of course, go ahead and read all this information to get all the details. But what I want to do now is to jump right into a very simple example in which I'm going to connect my HP 32 to my computer wirelessly using classic Bluetooth. And this example is one that comes with the Arduino and HP three to core. And it's going to file examples and let's see Bluetooth serial right here and bring this one up. So we want a serial to serial Bluetooth. So what we call the sketch is first that we include the Bluetooth serial library and then inside the setup function in line 16, we begin the Y, yet use P serial interface, as we always do when we want to use the serial monitor. And in line 17 we call the begin function and the serial city class Bluetooth class and pass a name. This is a name that will appear in my Bluetooth list when I search for the device that I want to connect to. So you can see I could begin for the USB serial interface, a wired USB studio interface, and going to begin class as well for the classic Bluetooth radio. The face inside the loop. We use the right command for the serial to the face and the red command for the USB serial wired face to send some data back and forth.

```
8
9 #if !defined(CONFIG_BT_ENABLED) || !defined(CONFIG_BLUEDROID_ENABLED)
10 #error Bluetooth is not enabled! Please run `make menuconfig` to and enable it
11 #endif
12
13 BluetoothSerial SerialBT;
14
15 void setup() {
16   Serial.begin(115200);
17   SerialBT.begin("ESP32test"); //Bluetooth device name
18   Serial.println("The device started, now you can pair it with bluetooth!");
19 }
20
21 void loop() {
22   if (Serial.available()) {
23     SerialBT.write(Serial.read());
24   }
25   if (SerialBT.available()) {
26     Serial.write(SerialBT.read());
27   }
28   delay(20);
29 }
```

So we use serial bitrate right now to send some data from the device to use the Bluetooth device. In this case the HP three goes back to the computer that is connected to via serial radio interface. So it's as simple as that. What I'll do is I will upload the sketch. Then after the upload is complete, I'm going to connect my computer to the computer via serial Bluetooth at this time, not serial use P like that. And then we'll just send some text characters back and forth. All right. So that is done. And then I'm going to bring up the serial monitor. But this is weird. All right. Very good. And so the device is started. You can now pair it with Bluetooth. That's going to my Bluetooth If we get up here and open up the Bluetooth preferences somewhere here, I'll see the Speaker two appearing advertising itself. We can name it P3 to test. Let's see the computer still trying to discover this new interface and they need to toggle Bluetooth on and off. I turn off Bluetooth on my computer and turn it back on so you can see the Bluetooth classic. It's not very fast. So on the contrary, DLP is lightning fast, as you'll see later. Look, I have to wait at all in between connections, all right? Just toggling the Bluetooth interface on my computer off and back on again. Consider the ESP three to test and a Bluetooth device appears something you connect to it and now it is connected. So I'm going to leave the serial interface that we use to be the wired interface that appears here because I'm going to use it and I'm going to bring up another serial monitor. I'm going to use an application called Serial Tools for this serial, which is pretty good because it allows me to create multiple sessions, multiple serial sessions, and each of these sessions can be connected to a different serial port, whether that is radio or wired, it doesn't matter as long as it's a serial port. So here I've got a single session up. I'm going to choose the ESP Ferry to test the serial port and then click on the Connect button to connect to it. All right. Now I'm going to send some data to my ISP 52 via the USB serial port and just say hello from the USB and then send it. All right. And you can see that the text, the string that I typed in to my serial use, the serial monitor was transmitted via USB to my ISP three to and then is three to send it back to me via Bluetooth.

Since this is where this session is connected to. It's connected to the Bluetooth Syria port and it bounced it back to me. I can also try to type some text into the Bluetooth session which will be transmitted wirelessly to the HP Theater. Two will pick it and send it back to my computer via the USB cable. So let's try again. Hello? Yes, P3 two. And that came back instantly, as you can see here. And there is a little example then of how you can use the USB three two Bluetooth classic capability to communicate with your computer wirelessly. So what I'm going to do in the next project is I'm going to connect this LCD screen. We say Hi script, see interface on it on my breadboard, so that any text that comes to the USB three via Bluetooth is displayed on the screen. And then I'm going to connect the USB cable, I'm going to power the HP 3 to 5 battery instead of the USB cable and therefore have the computer and the HP three two totally disconnected. And the only means of communication will be the Bluetooth classic radio. Let's try that out next.

BLUETOOTH CLASSIC PROJECT DEMONSTRATION

All right. In this project, I'm going to give you a small demonstration of an example application that you can build around Bluetooth Classic with your HP three two. We're going to show you how the gadget that you have got set up already here works. And then we can go through the details in this kit itself. So obviously you can see the ESP 32 here. I've got the HP three connected. How is it by a battery so it's not tethered to my computer via USB anymore. And that's because I want to show you how we can exclusively use the Bluetooth interface to communicate between my computer and the catch. I also have a nice square C LCD display connected. Plus I decided to put in a sense so we can get data from the sensor sent back to my computer wirelessly. So I've already connected the four, I have uploaded the firmware and then I have connected the USB three to my computer via Bluetooth. And you can see that it's name is expected to be a display and it's connected. And I'm using serial tools to set this serial port to this one here, which appears after I've connected the gadget to my computer, the rest are pretty much defaults. So the speed two beats imperative, etc. I left everything as default. The only thing that I've unchecked in this client is the raw option.

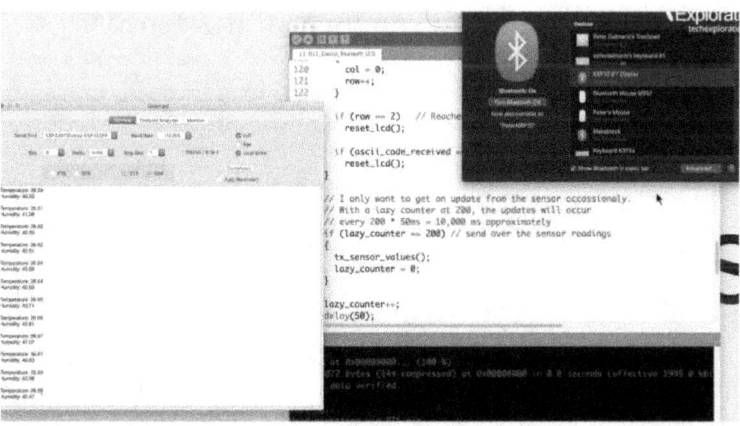

So I prefer to get the ASCII version of the characters instead of the real version. So as you can see, every 10 seconds or so the gadget will send the readings from the sensor back to my computer via the Bluetooth interface.

And more interestingly, if I type something on my keyboard to just show that you can see, let's say I'm going to type something like hello from the computer and some typing the character is each character at a time will be sent over to the HP 32 via the wireless interface and will appear in the LCD screen. And if I go for more characters that reach the end of the screen, which is the end of the second line real estate, then the screen is cleared and I can start typing from the top. So most characters seem to work at least anything that is ASCII will just work. If I want to clear the screen at any time, I can just type the tilde button or get killed. The character and the screen will clear. And at the same time, of course, the PSP 32 will send updates with the latest readings of the sensor.

BLUETOOTH CLASSIC PROJECT, DISPLAY MANAGEMENT

So now that you know what this gadget does, let's have a look at the sketch to learn more about how it does it. So here's a sketch. And of course, the components that you already know how to connect to your SB three two from previous projects in the library listed here. The only thing that's new compared to things that you've done in the past with these peripherals is that now we use the Bluetooth serial interface and you can actually learn more about the serial interface by going to the source code of the s p 32 to I code library. Have a look at the Bluetooth serial page file and you'll see the various functions that are available. In particular in this example, I'm using the right function and also this overloaded write function which has a pointer to an array of characters. It was a part the size of the cactus and the size of this array, I should say.

```
#if defined(CONFIG_BT_ENABLED) && defined(CONFIG_BLUEDROID_ENABLED)

#include "Arduino.h"
#include "Stream.h"
#include <esp_spp_api.h>

class BluetoothSerial: public Stream
{
    public:

        BluetoothSerial(void);
        ~BluetoothSerial(void);

        bool begin(String localName=String());
        int available(void);
        int peek(void);
        bool hasClient(void);
        int read(void);
        size_t write(uint8_t c);
        size_t write(const uint8_t *buffer, size_t size);
        void flush();
        void end(void);
        esp_err_t register_callback(esp_spp_cb_t * callback);

    private:
        String local_name;

};

#endif
```

So I'm also using what I'm still looking to browse on. I'm also looking at the information in this table here. This is the ASCII code table so that we learned, for example, that the code for the tool, the character, it's somewhere here, you know, down here, there it is. So the binary of the decimal code for the tilde character that I'm using to clear the LCD is 126. And remember this number, I'll be using it inside my sketch at some point in order to detect the very appropriate keystroke and clear the screen. So I've noted the euros for those two pages in the source code so we can make quick reference to them. So let's have a look at what's happening. We set up the sensors and the liquid crystal display set up in this serial Bluetooth pointer or hand. And I should say the object I've got a counter here, a laser counter that is the way by which I can get the P 32 to refresh the temperature and humidity readings and send them back to the computer at intervals of about 10 seconds each.

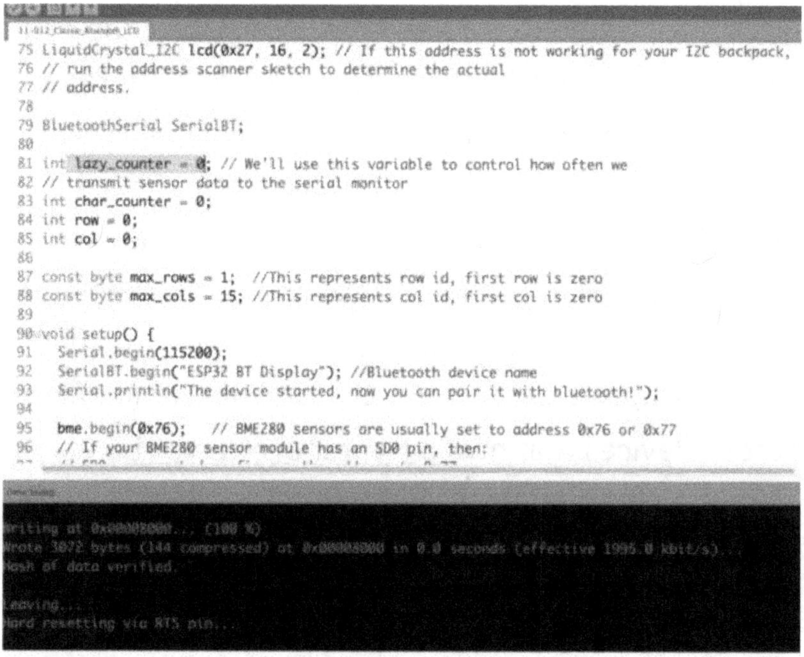

```
LiquidCrystal_I2C lcd(0x27, 16, 2); // If this address is not working for your I2C backpack,
// run the address scanner sketch to determine the actual
// address.

BluetoothSerial SerialBT;

int lazy_counter = 0; // We'll use this variable to control how often we
// transmit sensor data to the serial monitor
int char_counter = 0;
int row = 0;
int col = 0;

const byte max_rows = 1;  //This represents row id, first row is zero
const byte max_cols = 15; //This represents col id, first col is zero

void setup() {
  Serial.begin(115200);
  SerialBT.begin("ESP32 BT Display"); //Bluetooth device name
  Serial.println("The device started, now you can pair it with bluetooth!");

  bme.begin(0x76);    // BME280 sensors are usually set to address 0x76 or 0x77
  // If your BME280 sensor module has an SD0 pin, then:
```

```
riting at 0x00008000... (100 %)
rote 3072 bytes (144 compressed) at 0x00008000 in 0.0 seconds (effective 1995.0 kbit/s)...
ash of data verified.

eaving...
ard resetting via RTS pin...
```

That was just a quick and easy, therefore lazy way to do this sort of thing without using any blocking and without using an interrupt. I just wanted to keep this sketch as simple as possible so you'll see later how the music counter works is very simple. So I'm using this counter alongside with the row and column variables to manage the LCD screen and therefore calculate where to print the next character that arrives from the computer. These are constants. This is the size of my LCD. If I had an LCD screen of a different size like three rows, for example, in 15 columns, and it would have made this different, just notice that this is a zero based index. So if I say max rose equals one, it means that we have two rows with ID zero or index zero, I should say, and index one. Okay, the first row is zero. First row. Our first column is zero. Therefore we've got 16 available columns and two available rows. In this setup. We start the serial interface, even though I'm not using it in this example. And most importantly, we started the new Bluetooth interface and this is the name that I chose to use for this interface, and that is the name that you see appearing here on my list. This world of the Bluetooth devices that my computer can see or is connected to. And as usual, we'll start the sensor with the LCD screen and then we get into the loop.

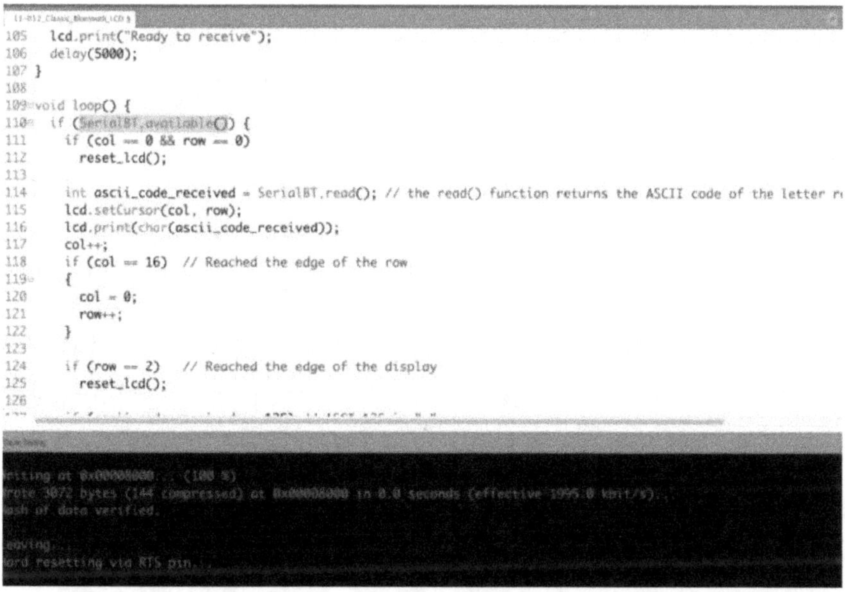

```
  lcd.print("Ready to receive");
  delay(5000);
}

void loop() {
  if (SerialBT.available()) {
    if (col == 0 && row == 0)
      reset_lcd();

    int ascii_code_received = SerialBT.read(); // the read() function returns the ASCII code of the letter r
    lcd.setCursor(col, row);
    lcd.print(char(ascii_code_received));
    col++;
    if (col == 16)  // Reached the edge of the row
    {
      col = 0;
      row++;
    }

    if (row == 2)   // Reached the edge of the display
      reset_lcd();
```

```
riting at 0x00008000... (100 %)
rote 3072 bytes (144 compressed) at 0x00008000 in 0.0 seconds (effective 1995.0 kbit/s)...
ash of data verified.

eaving...
ard resetting via RTS pin...
```

So in the loop we check constantly for new bytes that are available in the serial Bluetooth interface. And if there are new bytes available, then we use this code here to write those bytes onto the screen. So if column and row variables are zero and zero, it means that they've been reset recently or that we have cleared the screen recently, then we want to reset the LCD. So we call the reset LCD function, which is simply zeros. There's two variables and then the display is cleared. And these variables can also be reset and turned to zero from other parts of the sketch. And that's why I'm able to check for this condition here. So we've got a new LCD screen so cleared then because we've got a new byte waiting in this serial buffer to be read, we'll just go ahead and read it. So the read function returns this and says here, the ASCII code of the letter that I just typed on the keyboard. So I store this ASCII code in an integer. Then I set the cursor to the next location where I want to print this new character and in line 116, I print out this character on the LCD screen. So use print. Here's the code that I received. This is the ASCII code that we received by Bluetooth and with the car function, I convert this ASCII code into a character to print out.

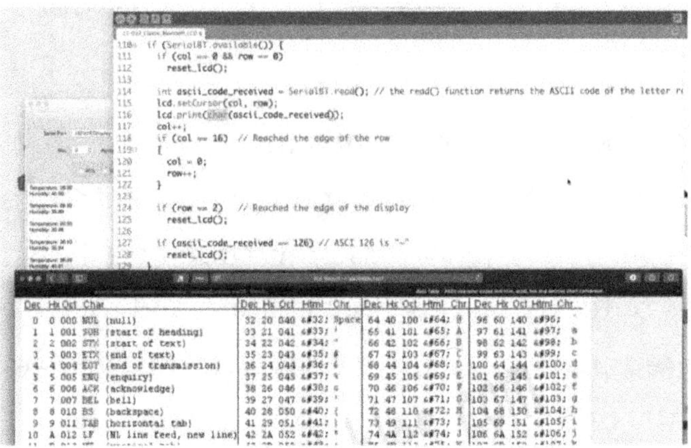

So let's say that I type in a just going to go and type another A here, it appears on the screen the lowercase a character is 97. Therefore this function will convert the 97 ASCII code into the character No case A and then will increase the column by one so that the next character will be printed on the next column. Whether it is the first row or the second row, it doesn't matter. But we know it's going to be the next column. If we have reached if we actually exceeded the number of columns available. So here I've got 16. But if I want to make this bit more parameterized, I know that we've got this variable here. I can just say if this is larger than this. So we have exceeded the number of columns available in each row, then make this a zero, make the column index of zero and increase the row by one. And if the row has exceeded the number of rows, Sarah available, equal either two or let's make that again parameter list slight improvements as we go. If that becomes larger than the available rows, then we call the reset LCD, which you have already seen. Now how do we clear the display? We check to see if the ASCII code that we received is 126 because point 26, as I said earlier, is the decimal code for the tilde sign or the tilde character. So we check for tilde and if we have a field that type, then we reset the LCD and that's all there is to do in order to write a copy. Everything that we type in the serial monitor here on to the LCD screen.

BLUETOOTH CLASSIC PROJECT, SENSOR UPDATES

Now take a look at the letter counter to say that this is a quick way to send the data from the sensor back to the Syria monitor. And they didn't want to use a blocking method here using delay and just decided to use a variable every time that it would go through the loop, increasing the variable by one set from zero because they wanted to do three. As soon as it reaches 200, we can go inside this block. Quality accesses values, which is this function here. We can come back to the minute and then zero later count dash and then we can start counting for the next period. Okay, let's check out what's happening inside the text sensor values, which is also quite interesting. So remember that our objective here is to get readings from the sensor and send them to the client or to the connected divider device, I should say to the client.

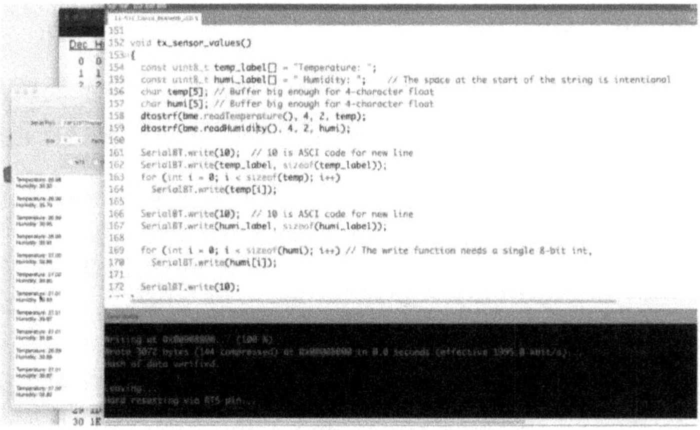

It's a device connected by the Bluetooth interface and prints it there. So that's how we get this text here, temperature number and humidity in the number. So that happens here. Should have quite a few writing statements. This one right statement here, this one here, like 161 164, 66 and so on. So here you can see both overloaded right functions and this great function here simply will send out the ASCII code for whatever images that we want to send. So I want to send, for example, a return line feed character, a special character line, feed, new line, essentially. And do that, I'm sending the decimal ASCII code, which is ten according to this table. So every time that we send a ten, we get a new line. You can see there's a new line here, there's a new line here. All those new lines are created because I sent out ten ASCII codes using the right function. So this one here in line 161 and this one here I 66 and one down here, since I've got three lines going over. So that's the first variant. The second variant is this one here in the source code, it's this. So as far as the parameters are concerned, we need to send a pointer to a byte array, which is also constant and also this size for this bright array.

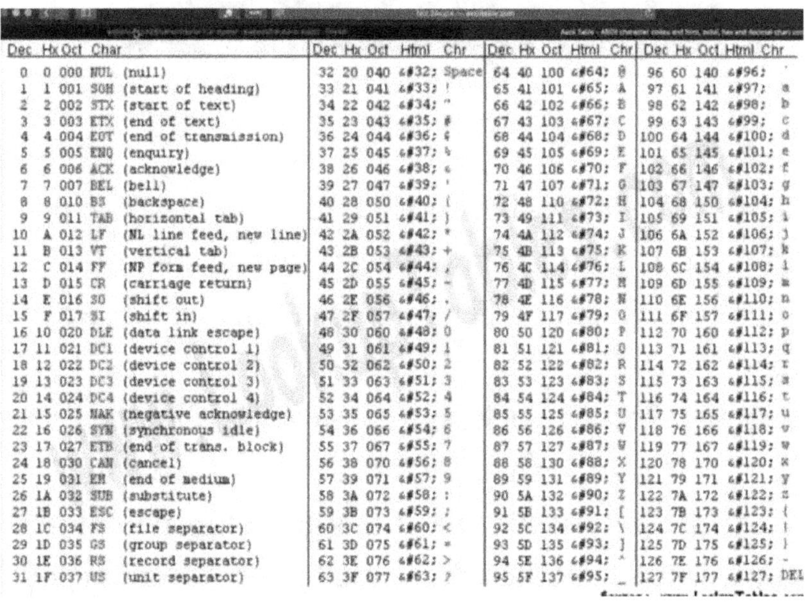

Dec	Hx	Oct	Char		Dec	Hx	Oct	Html	Chr	Dec	Hx	Oct	Html	Chr	Dec	Hx	Oct	Html	Chr
0	0	000	NUL	(null)	32	20	040		Space	64	40	100	@	@	96	60	140	`	`
1	1	001	SOH	(start of heading)	33	21	041	!	!	65	41	101	A	A	97	61	141	a	a
2	2	002	STX	(start of text)	34	22	042	"	"	66	42	102	B	B	98	62	142	b	b
3	3	003	ETX	(end of text)	35	23	043	#	#	67	43	103	C	C	99	63	143	c	c
4	4	004	EOT	(end of transmission)	36	24	044	$	$	68	44	104	D	D	100	64	144	d	d
5	5	005	ENQ	(enquiry)	37	25	045	%	%	69	45	105	E	E	101	65	145	e	e
6	6	006	ACK	(acknowledge)	38	26	046	&	&	70	46	106	F	F	102	66	146	f	f
7	7	007	BEL	(bell)	39	27	047	'	'	71	47	107	G	G	103	67	147	g	g
8	8	010	BS	(backspace)	40	28	050	(	(	72	48	110	H	H	104	68	150	h	h
9	9	011	TAB	(horizontal tab)	41	29	051	)	)	73	49	111	I	I	105	69	151	i	i
10	A	012	LF	(NL line feed, new line)	42	2A	052	*	*	74	4A	112	J	J	106	6A	152	j	j
11	B	013	VT	(vertical tab)	43	2B	053	+	+	75	4B	113	K	K	107	6B	153	k	k
12	C	014	FF	(NP form feed, new page)	44	2C	054	,	,	76	4C	114	L	L	108	6C	154	l	l
13	D	015	CR	(carriage return)	45	2D	055	-	-	77	4D	115	M	M	109	6D	155	m	m
14	E	016	SO	(shift out)	46	2E	056	.	.	78	4E	116	N	N	110	6E	156	n	n
15	F	017	SI	(shift in)	47	2F	057	/	/	79	4F	117	O	O	111	6F	157	o	o
16	10	020	DLE	(data link escape)	48	30	060	0	0	80	50	120	P	P	112	70	160	p	p
17	11	021	DC1	(device control 1)	49	31	061	1	1	81	51	121	Q	Q	113	71	161	q	q
18	12	022	DC2	(device control 2)	50	32	062	2	2	82	52	122	R	R	114	72	162	r	r
19	13	023	DC3	(device control 3)	51	33	063	3	3	83	53	123	S	S	115	73	163	s	s
20	14	024	DC4	(device control 4)	52	34	064	4	4	84	54	124	T	T	116	74	164	t	t
21	15	025	NAK	(negative acknowledge)	53	35	065	5	5	85	55	125	U	U	117	75	165	u	u
22	16	026	SYN	(synchronous idle)	54	36	066	6	6	86	56	126	V	V	118	76	166	v	v
23	17	027	ETB	(end of trans. block)	55	37	067	7	7	87	57	127	W	W	119	77	167	w	w
24	18	030	CAN	(cancel)	56	38	070	8	8	88	58	130	X	X	120	78	170	x	x
25	19	031	EM	(end of medium)	57	39	071	9	9	89	59	131	Y	Y	121	79	171	y	y
26	1A	032	SUB	(substitute)	58	3A	072	:	:	90	5A	132	Z	Z	122	7A	172	z	z
27	1B	033	ESC	(escape)	59	3B	073	;	;	91	5B	133	[	[	123	7B	173	{	{
28	1C	034	FS	(file separator)	60	3C	074	<	<	92	5C	134	\	\	124	7C	174			|
29	1D	035	GS	(group separator)	61	3D	075	=	=	93	5D	135	]	]	125	7D	175	}	}
30	1E	036	RS	(record separator)	62	3E	076	>	>	94	5E	136	^	^	126	7E	176	~	~
31	1F	037	US	(unit separator)	63	3F	077	?	?	95	5F	137	_	_	127	7F	177		DEL

So let's see a couple of ways by which we can use that. First of all, here's an example where I want to send out just the text. Temperature and humidity is what appears here, temperature and humidity. So to do that, first I create a constant eight bit array of characters. I give it a name and I initialize it with this content. I've got a space here as well, deliberately so that I can align it properly right under the temperature t of the temperature. And then I take each of these and have a look at line 162. I provide it to the overloaded version of the right function right here. And then I use the size of the function. I just see a function that gives me the number of bytes. I'll show you the number of cells that are in this array, which is equivalent to the number of bytes in this array as needed by this write function. So line 162 will print out this text in a Bluetooth serial monitor and then do the same thing down here in line 167, which does the same thing. But for the humidity label, which is this. So that will print out humidity right there, then I need to do the same thing for the temperature and humidity values. However, these values change. So I can create a constant array with those values. It has to be I have to use the first version of the right function, which is this one here. This right function requires an input, a single character. So a byte in eight bytes. And of course here the temperature and humidity readings of type float, not of type byte are over an integer. So you can see what it looks like is not an integer, right? It's a floating point number. So I need a way to convert a floating point number that comes back from the sensor. When I use the read temperature and read humidity functions and convert that into an array of characters. And then I need to send each one of the bytes in the array of characters via the Bluetooth interface using the right function. So here, here's how I do that. First, I create a couple of buffers. These buffers are just temperature and humidity, character arrays, and each one has got five spots available, five five locations available. So I should say here, five and five because I need to take into account the delimiter for the decimals as well and the built here count as well. And that needs to be stored inside the array. So what we want to do is we can take the number that there is a need to read temperature returns, which is a number that contains decimals converted into a string that contains a total of four characters. Make sure that the last two characters are the decimals. So that tells us where the dot should go and then store that inside the temp buffer that I've created up here. And you can learn more about how the data string F function works by having a look at this little article here from Microchip. So once we do that, we've got the number with a decimal stored inside the temp and the humidity character arrays. That takes us to line 163 and 154 for the temperature printout. So because we can only write one bite at a time using the right function, we need to put the right function inside a loop. So inside this loop we count from zero index zero to index, whatever the total size of the temp character array is. And each time, right, the byte that is stored in that cell of the temp array to the Bluetooth interface. So first will take byte zero, send it out, and that is going to be number two. Then we'll take the one from the temp character array and send it over to the Bluetooth interface. And that is going to be number seven in this case, and then we're going to be three and so on until all of the contents of the array have been sent over, we're going to do exactly the same thing then for the humidity. So we're going to take one bite at a time, starting from zero, going all the way to five, and that we then transmit the full number that represents the value retrieved from the sensor via the Bluetooth interface. So I hope that this makes sense. However, I could look at it just by walking through it manually to understand how it works and then also use the resources that I've got up here to understand more about how they ask you how our code works and just edit the URL to the article about the two strings. F Okay, so I hope that this makes sense. Let's move on to the next project now where we'll start playing around with Bluetooth. Low energy. Barely.

BLE SERVER (PART 1)

Hi. In this project, I'm going to give you a crash course or a quick introduction to barely Bluetooth. Low energy. I'm going to explain what Bella is in terms of its functionality and then how we can use Billy to build simple applications. And I want to start by having a look at a very simple application that a lot of you are probably familiar with. So what if God right here is a heart rate monitor? It's obviously a device. What it does is that it measures my heart rate and then it sends it out to a client, like in this case, my phone or some other device. It can connect to it so that I can get a reading of this heart rate measured by the server. So I've already mentioned a couple of terms here. This thing here is the server.

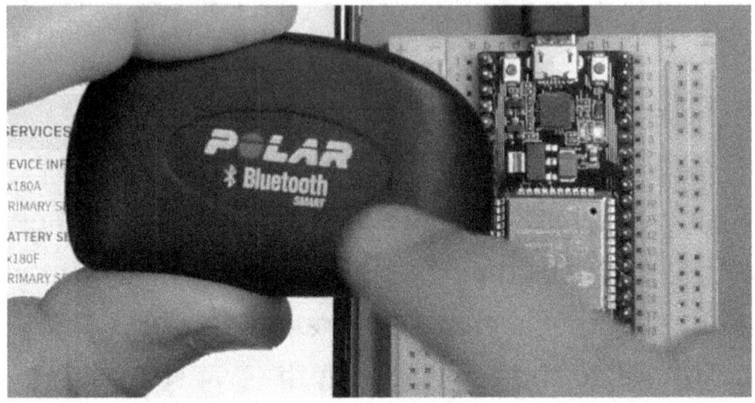

It's the thing that generates the data that it sends to a client for the client to display on a screen or record in a database or use in some other way. So already you know that in Bali we've got clients and we've got service. The nice thing about the belly is that it's very light wind energy, as the name says, and such a very lightweight protocol. So it's very fast. And those small amounts of data can move from server to client very quickly. Connections are also very fast. You don't need to go through a full pairing process like we did in the previous projects with Bluetooth Classic. So essentially you just look for a device, you tap on a button and you plug it in and you connect. As I'm going to show you in a minute,

I'm going to plug this back onto this drop that I've got around my waist so that it can start sending some heart rate values to my phone. And I'm going to extend a few other things about how data is organized in VLA. Okay, so the monitor struck back on to my waist or my chest, I should say, and let's pick it up again. So here it is. It appears actually one step back. I'm using this little app called Belly Scanner, and I've got links to this application for Android and iOS. In my sketch, a sample sketch that I will be looking at later. So here it is. There's a lot of applications like that for smartphones that allow you to play around with daily devices. But I found that this one is really, really good, as you'll see.

So I've started the application, the application scans around for any belly devices that it can pick up. And here's the polar H7 server that is running inside my heart rate monitor. And apart from that, I'm here. You see my ESP32 service, which is right now running on my ESP 32 and I'm going to come back to that later. First, let's connect to the polar H7 device. So I've just connected the services to the device, I should say the server running on the device. And it's a bunch of bits of information here. So that's the advertisement data, the name of the device that we just connected to information about the manufacturer and other bits and pieces. But down here, which is very important for us and for the projects that will follow with good information about the available services. So a quick look at the gut profile hierarchy. Don't worry too much about what the gap is and all that, but what I want you to focus on this thing here, kick the orange box. So the orange box is called a characteristic. And think of it as a box or a container that contains properties and a value in the value is what your belly server wants to send to transmit to a client. Like my phone. And above that, the next level up in the hierarchy is a service. So a service can contain multiple characteristics and a device can contain multiple services. So you can see one large box here and then there's another one on the right side. And there's three dots indicating that you can have an arbitrary number of services running on a server.

GATT Profile Hierarchy

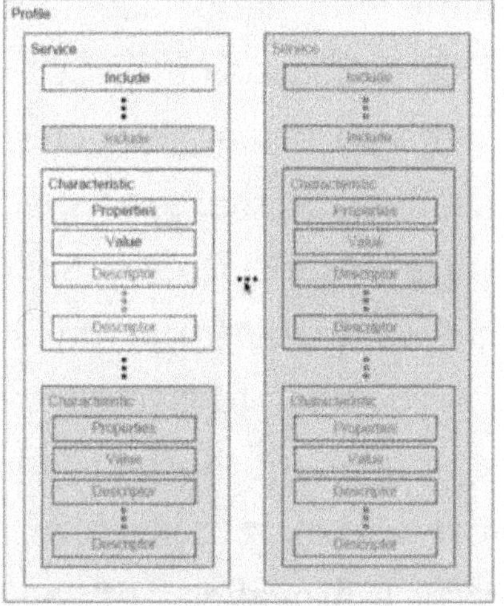

The top level of the hierarchy is a profile, which is composed of one or more services necessary to fulfill a use case. A service is composed of characteristics or references to other services. A characteristic consists of a type (represented

Each of the services can have multiple properties and one to value that they are to be communicated with a client. So back to my polar H7 example, you can see here down and the service says we've got one, two, three, four different services. One of them is a battery service. So it's telling us about the charge on the battery inside the device at 70%. This thing here is the value and it comes xrx a decimal value, but also as a percentage. The application here, the client interprets that. And another important thing to notice here is this idea. This is a specific idea that the Bluetooth consortium has allocated to this particular kind of characteristic, this particular kind of container for data to a19. Now, let's have a look. Can go to the page called got characteristics that I've got a link to here in the information segment of my sketch and it says right here, this is a euro you want to go to and I can search for this particular characteristic a day to a19, and it's this one here. So there is a specific allocated I.D for the battery level specification. So if you're building a gadget that wants to provide this kind of information to a client, then you need to give it this specific ID or utility. We'll talk more about those in a minute so that the client knows what kind of data this server with this characteristic is providing. Let's go back one level. Have a look at the heart rate, which is something more interesting at this point in time. So this is another characteristic that my heart rate monitor is transmitting and its idea is to a37. So if we plug that into my search box here to a three, it's seven and you'll see that this characteristic is a heart rate measurement characteristic. If we drill in it and get more information about how this value is transmitted, what are the contents of the components, I should say, of this value? And we can see that there's one byte or eight bits that make up the flags and it's additional information here. The first bit to zero is a heart rate value for the page. There's some information here about the definition of this and what it does and next to it, it's the sense of contacts and so on. And the next eight bits, the actual value of the as the actual heart rate value that this characteristic contains. It's an eight bit word. So it's a single byte, an eight bit integer, and it's this value here that you can see right now 85 degrees. But this hexadecimal version of the value is this one here. This is the raw value and it consists of these eight bits for the flags. Another eight bits for the heart rate measurement, valid values, sorry, and another 16 bits, which is also the heart rate measurement value. But now a 16 bit representation of it. And then we've got another 16 bits about the expended energy. So you can guess how many kilojoules have been expended so far. And finally we've got the R interval, another 16 bits. So all of this put together to transmit it as one single value right here. The client will just take the second byte and convert that into a decimal and display it here. And this is something that will be doing as well in one of the example applications later on in this section. So now I want to go back a couple of levels and connect to my ESP32 because I want to show you a couple of things here. It's connected to the ESP 32 and you can see that it's got a new ID which looks very different to the idea of the or to the address of the heart rate monitor. I just quickly go back and have a look at I.D. four heart rate monitors, totally different. So this is a guide for the device, a unique device. So every device has got a unique 128 bit ID, we call that a unity and that really depends on the hardware. We can't change it. And below that we've got the EU IDs for the services and then the characteristics like that. So we've got three levels of IDs. Each of those is unique.

Now the ones that we have control over. Let's go back to my ISP 32, the ones that we have control over, those that have to do with the services and the characteristics. So you did these generated by the hardware, but the rest we can control. So let's have a look. We've got a custom service here and here is the UID for that custom service. And then I've got two characteristics under that service. Here is the user ID for the first characteristic and the EU ID for the second characteristic. And then inside these characteristics we've got the values. So the first value, the value for the first characteristic, has a world car, one for characteristic one and the value for the second characteristic is this. Hello World Car two. So at this point we know that a device may have multiple services, each service may have multiple characteristics, each characteristic service and device has unique IDs and in particular the device EU IDs really depend on the hardware we can't control. We can't change, but we have control over the EU IDs for the services and for the characteristics. So we said, I'm going to move on now to the next part of this project. Where are we going to go through this example sketch and see how we can create custom services and characteristics on the edge, be fitted to that. Then we can go onto our client, in this case my phone and interact with them.

BLE SERVER (PART 2)

So let's continue by having a look at the sketch that is running right now. My P32 provides me with a service that contains two characteristics. All right. So we start by including the necessary libraries. We've got the device on top of it, which could be in the utils and to be at least server. Since this is what we are trying to build. Below that, I need to define the UI ds for the service and then for the two characteristics that this service contains. These ideas are essentially randomly generated, but because they are 828 bits each, there is a very, very good chance that it is unique and that there is no other service or characteristic or device on the planet that has the same UI. D. I generated the UI via this online tool. Just go to this location. You uid generate a dot net.

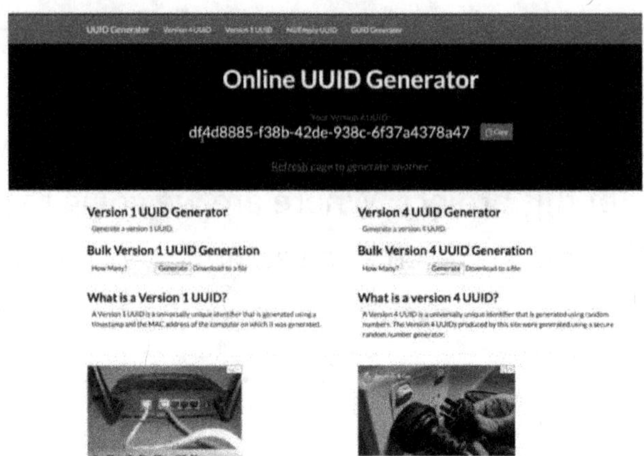

Just refresh the page and each time you refresh the page you get a new UI to just simply copy that into my sketch and I get three of those. So end up with three unique user IDs. So now that I've got the UI IDs, I'm going to skip those pages and go to the setup function. In the setup function, I use the complete function of the device class to create the new device handle and I give it a name my ESP 32 and that can be arbitrary. So this is a name that appears here in my scanner, my SB 30. That's how I can identify my Billie device running with the HB 32. Among other things. A lot of other devices with their own different names. So you can put your name here as if you like.

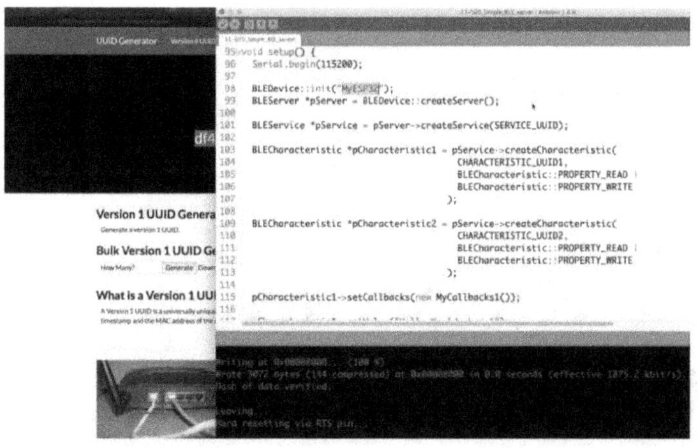
UUID Generator
Version 1 UUID Genera
Bulk Version 1 UUID Ge
What is a Version 1 UUI
void setup() {
Serial.begin(115200);
BLEDevice::init("MyESP32");
BLEServer *pServer = BLEDevice::createServer();
BLEService *pService = pServer->createService(SERVICE_UUID);
BLECharacteristic *pCharacteristic1 = pService->createCharacteristic(
CHARACTERISTIC_UUID1,
BLECharacteristic::PROPERTY_READ |
BLECharacteristic::PROPERTY_WRITE
);
BLECharacteristic *pCharacteristic2 = pService->createCharacteristic(
CHARACTERISTIC_UUID2,
BLECharacteristic::PROPERTY_READ |
BLECharacteristic::PROPERTY_WRITE
);
pCharacteristic1->setCallbacks(new MyCallbacks1());

Then I create a server valley server and this is the pointer to the handle that server below that I create a service go service and can have multiple services as you like. In this example, I only have one service. Do that by calling the create service function on the server. And then I remember I want to create two characteristics that are part of this service. So I use the create characteristic function that is part of the P service object, and I pass a bunch of parameters which are the UI for the service that I want to create and then to properties that the service has. So I'm going to be able to read and write to this characteristic. And that's why here you can see that we've got read and write capabilities on this characteristic.

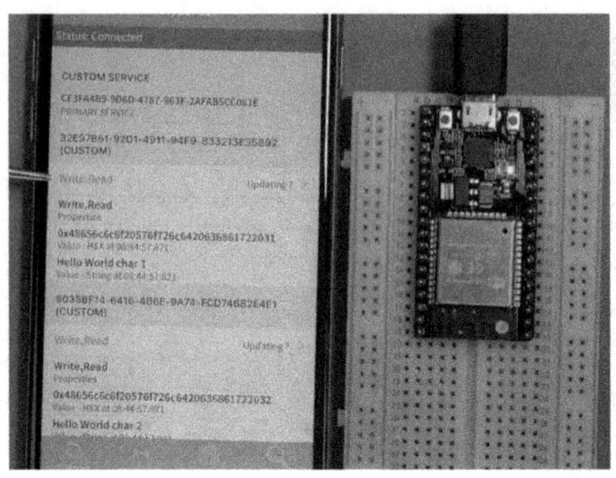

And later on I'm going to make some changes to the existing value by actually writing to the characteristic or to the minute. I do the exact same thing for the second characteristics of a different point on X characteristic two and then I create in the same way, create characteristics, pass the unique identifier, the UI d, and it also has the same properties for reading and writing. Then because we are creating a server here, we want this server to be able to react to a client changing the values of the characteristics. And this happens via callbacks. So here in line 1.5 I create the first callback for the first characteristic and then here in line 119, I create a callback for the second characteristic. So a callback is code that I've written up here, I've included up here. It's just an embedded class. I give it an arbitrary name. This one is what you got. What I've got highlighted here matches the name that you declared in the callbacks. Fine. Down here, this is going to work. But then what is inside the callback? Embedded class. This is specific. So we have the on right function or handler and then the on read, which I haven't got here because I don't have a handler for on read only. I'm only interested in doing something when the client is trying to make a change to the value of the characteristic. So that change is an on right event that will be handled by this code. And what this code does is first to get the value of the characteristic, the new value of the characteristic that the client has just typed in or entered, and then to print it out to the serial monitor.

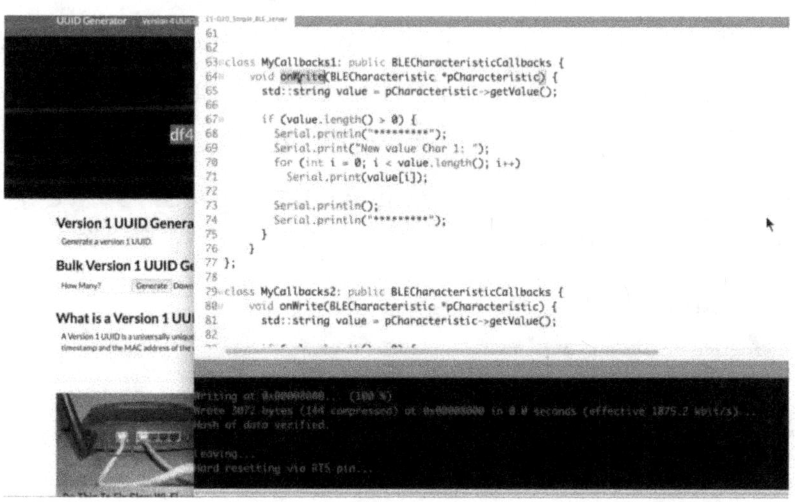

And you probably remember what is happening here from the previous project, the classic, the Bluetooth, the get the value function would say to the value that the client has written to this characteristic in an array of bytes, and then to print it out to the serial monitor, I need to take these bytes one at a time and send it out to the serial monitor. So here's the array and then we say square brackets. I can access and retrieve the value of each one of the cells in this array and then send it out to the serial monitor. And I'm doing the exact same thing here for the second callback. So once I set the callbacks, I can continue by writing at the default or the first value to the two characteristics. So Helloworld one and Helloworld car two. And that's what you see right here is the first value for the first characteristic and the first value for the second characteristic. And that actually changes those in a minute. So once we have the two characteristics set, we can start the service of which the two characteristics are part of and to make this be any service discoverable by a client, we need to start the advertising process so we create an advertising handle and then we start advertising.

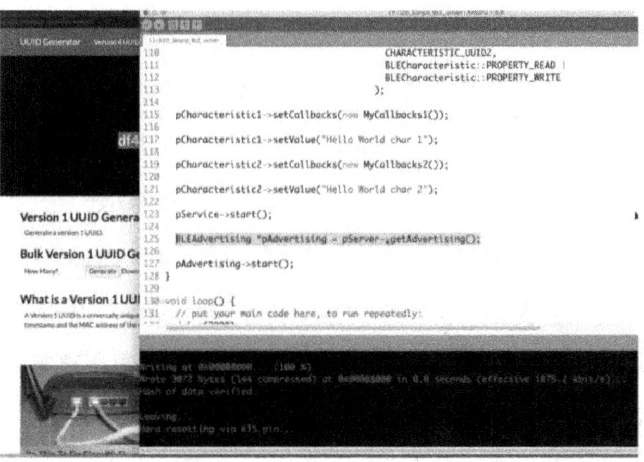

So now my two especially are starting to advertise, which means to broadcast to its environment that it's ready to receive a connection injury to connect with a client. That's all there is. We don't have anything in the loop because nothing is really happening in the loop. Everything is happening through the event handlers and the callbacks. So I'm going to bring up a serial monitor and I'm connected to my security via the USB interface. And what I'll do next, I'll leave that here so we can get a better view. What the next is, I'm going to change the values that the two characteristics currently contain. So let's write a new value, make it a text value, and make it something simple like this header and write that. All right. And you can see that in the serial monitor. The value hello also appeared. And then what you see here is the value handler in hexadecimal. Let's try one more thing. I'm going to write a value, but this time it's going to be a hexadecimal value instead of a text value. So let's say I want to send out a capital A to a Capital A's here in the ASCII table, and its hexadecimal code is 41. So when you type in 41 and see what happens, Right. Okay. So you can see that here is the new value 41 read value 41. So that is the latest value that is attracting. And the other ones here are historical previous values. And if I go back one level, you can see that a also appears here in the value of this characteristic. I do the same thing for the second one. So right value you can do right, say hexadecimal 41 And I'm also going to sentence another hex value for B, which is 42 and see what happens. Okay, so here is 41 and 42 and I'm going to read it and there's 4142 and I should probably not have it all right here because it is transmitted properly. It's recorded properly to hexadecimal values. When turned into text, they are a B correctly shown here. All right. So this was an example of a simple implementation of a bare server using custom characteristics instead of predefined by the Bluetooth consortium characteristics in the next project. What we'll do is I'm going to connect the LCD screen to my ESP 32 so that the values of the characteristics display on the LCD screen, instead of having to use my computer in the serial monitor and the USB connection to do so. In addition, in the next project I will have the ESP32 powered by a battery, so that it is not connected or tethered to my computer. But let's check it out.

BLE SERVER WITH LCD

Hi. In this project I have added a square LCD screen to my gadget that was used in the previous project in order to display the changes to the values of the two characteristics as they happened in my client. In other words, I've got the police server running on the ESP 32 and I've got my phone connected to it as a client. And every time I make a change to one of their characteristics, that change will be reflected on the screen. So let's show you how it works. So here's my ESP three to the elite server. I've called it Peter's ESP 32 Tap on the panic button to connect really quickly, much faster than the pairing process in the classic Bluetooth. So then I'm going to drill into customer services and I've got my two characteristics here.

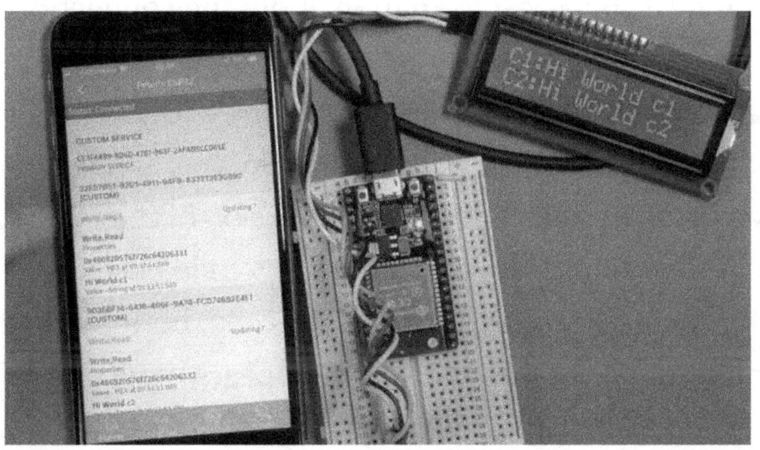

At the moment, the first characteristic has its default value, and here's the default value for the second characteristic. And it can also see those values on the LCD. And let's make a little change. I'll go to the first characteristic and just write a new value like one, two, three, four, two. Right? And the LCD screen is updated with a new value. If you tap it to read it, we'll see the hex version of the value here and I'll show here exactly as expected as expected as two. The same thing for the second characteristic, I'm going to write a new value to replace the existing one. I'm going to go for just normal text and make that A, B, C, D, and write here and there's C to A, B, C, D on the LCD screen that is the value in hex. And here's the value this will display in the client. So just a simple addition or very few modifications to this catch that we saw in the previous project to add the LCD screen to the mix. So let's have a look at the sketch to see how I've done this. So basic information about the connections or things that you already know. I haven't made any changes to the UUID here. I just added the LCD screen, the library and the object to control it. So the changes that I've made have to do with the inclusion of the LCD screen in the callbacks. I have added this code here to print the characters one character at a time, both to the serial monitor so you can see how it appears here, and also to the LCD screen. Again, picking a value from the character array and then sending it to the screen one at a time.

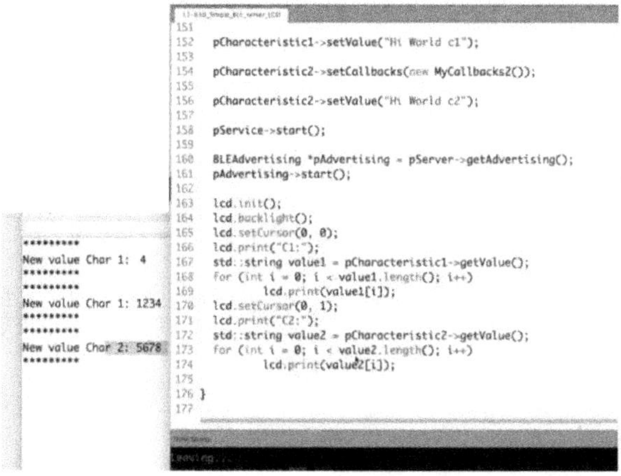

```
pCharacteristic1->setValue("Hi World c1");

pCharacteristic2->setCallbacks(new MyCallbacks2());

pCharacteristic2->setValue("Hi World c2");

pService->start();

BLEAdvertising *pAdvertising = pServer->getAdvertising();
pAdvertising->start();

lcd.init();
lcd.backlight();
lcd.setCursor(0, 0);
lcd.print("C1:");
std::string value1 = pCharacteristic1->getValue();
for (int i = 0; i < value1.length(); i++)
        lcd.print(value1[i]);
lcd.setCursor(0, 1);
lcd.print("C2:");
std::string value2 = pCharacteristic2->getValue();
for (int i = 0; i < value2.length(); i++)
        lcd.print(value2[i]);

}
```

```
*********
New value Char 1: 4
*********
*********
New value Char 1: 1234
*********
*********
New value Char 2: 5678
*********
```

And I've done the same thing to the second callback for the second characteristic. And the only change in the setup function again is the addition of the code for the LCD screen. On top of that, I am powering the P3 to get it by a battery so it's not connected to my computer. And then the whole communication with the client. My phone is wireless. So this is just a little example to see how easy it is to create custom services and custom characteristics and to be early application on your ISP. 32 But as I said in a previous project, another very interesting aspect of working with PLM is the ability to work with devices like this one, the heart rate monitor. There are temperature gauges and environmental sensors and lots of other devices that implement various body services with their characteristics.

www.ingramcontent.com/pod-product-compliance
Lightning Source LLC
LaVergne TN
LVHW051323050326
832903LV00031B/3329
* 9 7 9 8 3 0 0 5 2 0 6 9 4 *